AF269121

Paper Flower Crafts

2nd Edition

68 Paper Flowers You Can Use for Decorations, Card Accents, Scrapbooking, & Much More!

by Kitty Moore

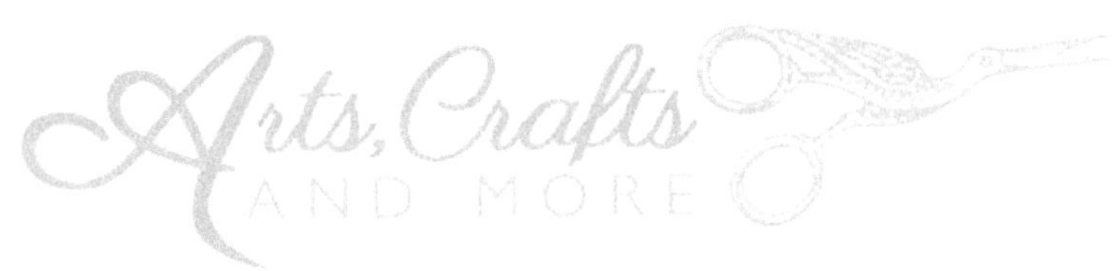

Copyright © 2017 By Kitty Moore
All rights reserved. No part of this book may be reproduced in any form
without permission in writing from the author. No part of this publication
may be reproduced or transmitted in any form or by any means, mechanic,
electronic, photocopying, recording, by any storage or retrieval system, or
transmitted by email without the permission in writing from the author and
publisher.
For information regarding permissions write to author at
kitty@artscraftsandmore.com.
Reviewers may quote brief passages in review.

Please note that credit for the images used in this book go to the respective
owners. You can view this at: ArtsCraftsAndMore.com/image-list

Kitty Moore
ArtsCraftsAndMore.com

Table of Contents

Introduction

Paper flowers are great and so much fun to make. Whether you want to liven up your greeting cards or embellish your scrapbook pages or simply create some fun and cheerful decorations, paper flowers are a quick solution– easy to make and very inexpensive. If you need a rainy-day project to keep your kids busy, this is a great activity that will keep them occupied for hours.

Paper flowers are so versatile and can be made out of just about any paper – from crepe paper to thick cardstock to recycled household products. Your imagination is the only limit to your creativity - you can make any type of flower you like – from simple daisies to magnificent roses. Origami flowers are a quick way to wow your friends as well.

This book is going to teach you how to make your own paper flowers step by step - starting out with basic flowers and working your way up to more complex flowers.

1. Cheerful Paper Daisies

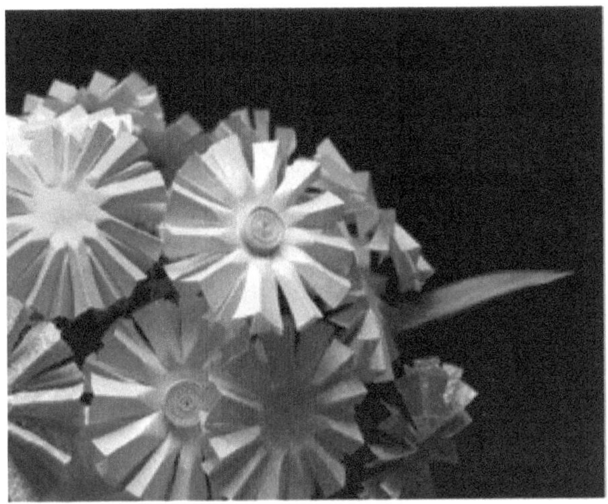

Materials

- Craft paper
- Scraps of yellow paper
- Hot glue gun
- Scissors
- Compass or lid of a jar (to size required)
- Pencil
- Ruler
- Floral wire
- Green floral wire
- Vase

Directions

1. Draw a circle that is 3" in circumference or trace the lid of a jar. Use this as your template. (3" circles will give you a more petit looking flower and 5" will make more of an impact). Trace the circles on the card and cut 2 circles.

2. Draw 8 x 1" lines evenly spaced around the circle. Cut along the lines. Fold the card in between each line and crease. The creases don't have to all be the same; some can be soft or hard or only part of the area. Follow the same steps with the other circle.

3. Place a dot of glue in the center of 1 circle and glue the other circle on top making sure that you see the petals of the bottom circle.

4. Cut a strip of yellow paper 1/8" wide by 18" long. Wind into a tight spiral disc and glue the ends closed. Glue the yellow disc to the middle of the flower.

5. Attach a piece of floral wire to the bottom of the flower and wrap with florist tape. Make as many daisies as you require using the steps above. Arrange your daisies in a vase and bring some cheer to your home.

2. Easy to Make Paper Hyacinths

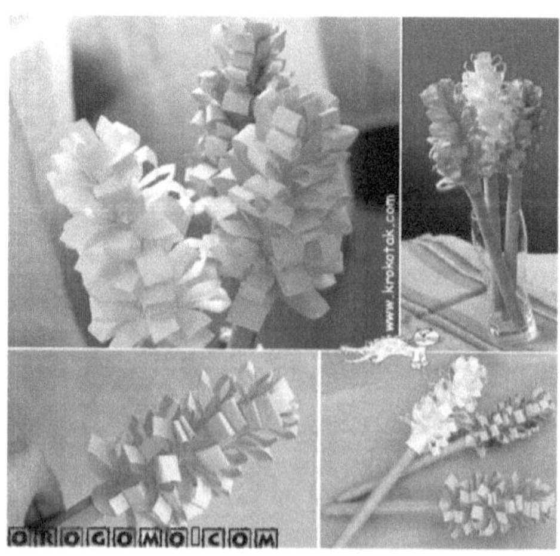

Materials

- Green paper
- Colored paper

- Glue
- Scissors

Directions

1. Roll up a piece of green paper (this will be the stem). Run a line of glue along the open edge and glue to the rest of the paper.

2. Divide an A4 piece of paper into 4 sections and cut. Fold the paper in half lengthwise. Cut evenly spaced strips along the folded side of the paper.

3. Glue the one edge and attach to the green stem. Wind the paper around the stem and secure with glue. Continue winding the rest of the paper down the stem as above. Fluff out the petals to add volume to the flower. dThis is a wonderful easy activity to keep your children busy on those rainy days.

3. Pretty Felt Hair Flowers

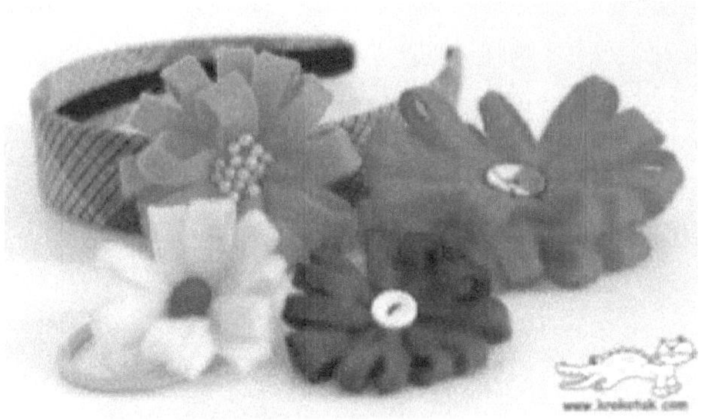

Materials

- Felt
- Buttons
- Scissors

- Needle and thread

Directions

1. Cut a piece of felt in a rectangle shape 3" wide by 15" long (vary the length according to the size of flower you want to make). Fold the felt in half lengthwise.

2. On the folded area, cut fringes of 1" in length. Keeping the felt folded, sew along the bottom of the felt. Pull the thread as you go until the two ends meet. You will now have a round flower shape. Sew the two edges together.

3. Attach a button to the center of the flower. You can make another flower to overlay the flower that has been made. If you want a bigger and fluffier flower to attach to a headband, then overlay two flowers. These pretty flowers can also be attached to any form of hair accessories.

4. Decorative Flowers for Christmas Lights

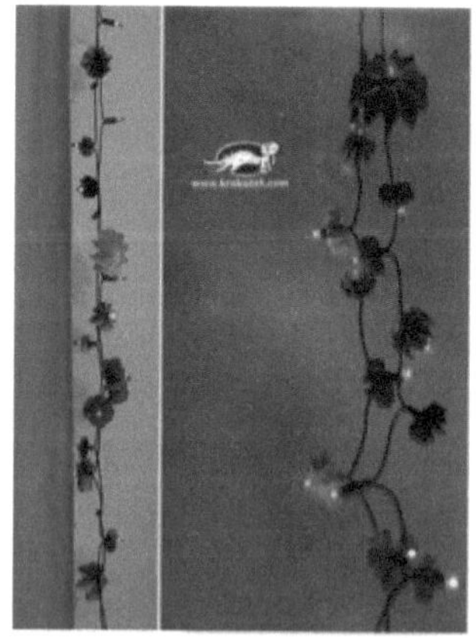

Materials

- Paper (in various colors)
- Glue
- Scissors

- Ruler

Directions

1. Cut 2 different color papers into strips of 1" wide. Place 1 color horizontally and glue the corner of the other piece of paper vertically.

2. Start to fold the 1st color strip over 2nd color strip and continue in this method until all the paper is folded. It will look like a concertina. There should be at least 10 to 12 folds for the flower to be elastic.

3. Glue the ends of the paper strips together. Finally glue the beginning and the end of the flower together. Make as many flowers as you need in different sizes and colors. Slip the Christmas lights through the flowers and switch on. You will be amazed at how beautifully the light dances on the different colored flowers.

5. Halloween Tulle Flowers

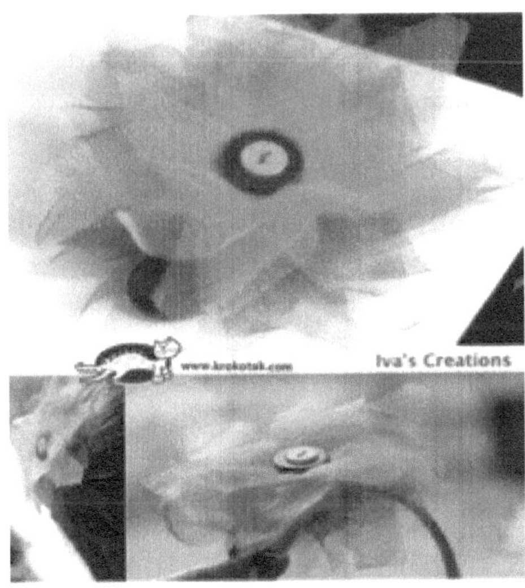

Materials

- Tulle (different colors)
- Beads
- Buttons
- Scissors
- Needle and thread
- Peg
- Silicone gun
- Hairpin
- Ruler
- Marker
- Paper

Directions

1. Measure and mark a 4" by 4" square on the paper and use this as the template. Cut 15-16 tulle squares from the template. You can place multiple layers of tulle together and then cut.

2. Fold the tulle in half and cut. Fold the pointed side of the tulle inwards towards the edge and hold together with a peg. Fold next piece of tulle and peg on top of the first folded piece of tulle. Hold together with a peg.

3. Continue to fold the other 13 pieces of tulle as above and secure each layer with the peg. Sew all the shapes together, smoothing out the tulle shapes to form the pattern of a flower.

4. Sew the button to the middle of the flower. The button can be decorated by gluing beads on the button.

5. Glue the flower to a hairpin or hairband. Painting scary faces for Halloween is the norm and together with the tulle flower your children will be the rave of the day.

I have included a bonus just for you…

FOR A LIMITED TIME ONLY – Get my best-selling book "DIY Crafts: The 100 Most Popular Crafts & Projects That Make Your Life Easier" absolutely FREE!

Readers who have downloaded the bonus book as well have seen the greatest changes in their crafting abilities and have expanded their repertoire of crafts – so it is *highly recommended* to get this bonus book today!

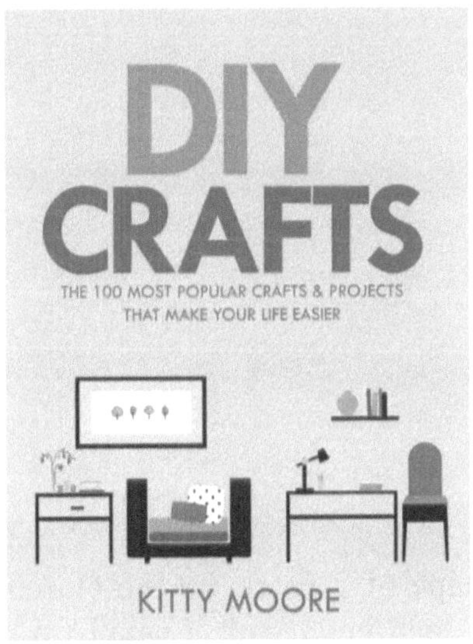

Get your free copy at:

ArtsCraftsAndMore.com/Bonus

6. Coffee Filter Roses

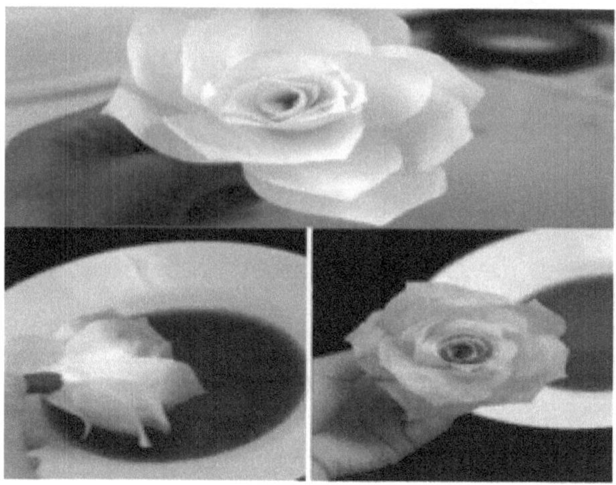

Materials

- Coffee filters
- Pencil
- Scissors
- Florist wire
- Florist tape
- Craft glue
- Food coloring

Directions

1. Draw the shape of 2 petals on the closed side of the coffee filter. Draw each petal with a small tip. Cut out the shape. Wind an inch of tape at the top of the florist wire. Gently prize open the closed bottom section of the coffee filter.

2. Starting with the first petal (there will be 4 in a row) wind them round the florist wire (center petals). Secure with florist tape. Cut the rest of the petal strips into individual petals.

3. Scrunch the bottom of the petal, add a spot of glue and place on the center petals. Continue to scrunch and attach petals, moving round the florist wire. Make sure that each petal slightly overlaps the previous petal.

4. Once you have added sufficient petals to give you a rose shape; secure the bottom with florist tape and continue to wind the tape down the length of the wire.

5. Dilute food coloring in some water and dip the rose into the coloring. The coffee filter will quickly absorb the dye. If you want to make the edges of the petals a different color, add more coloring to the water and dip only the edges of the petal into the coloring.

7. White Paper Anemones

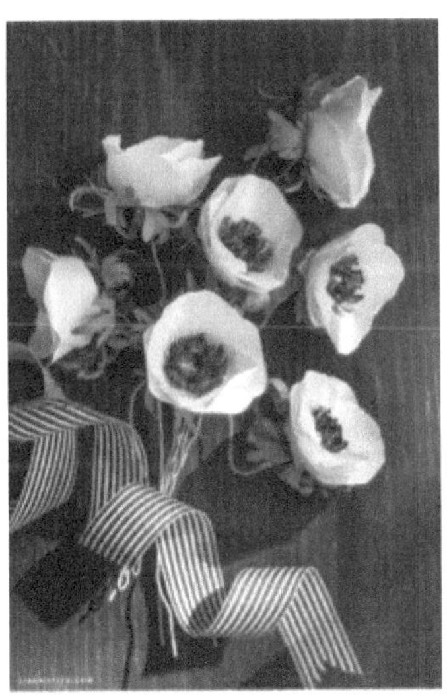

Materials

- White metallic paper
- Green card
- Black Metallic paper
- Florist wire

- Florist tape
- Scissors
- Paper
- Pencil
- Low temperature hot glue gun

Directions

1. On a piece of white paper, draw the shape of a shell for the petals (bottom flat); a 5-fringed leaf; a 6-pointed star and 2 round 1 ½" and 1" circles. These will be used as your templates.

2. Trace the 7 flower shapes and the star onto the white card. At the bottom edge of the petal cut 2 short slits. Curl the edges of the petals with the scissors. Overlap the outer edges of the slits and glue.

3. Glue together 1 set of 3 petals closing in the center. Glue together 1 set of 4 petals and close in the center. Glue the 3 petals shape to the bottom 4 petals. Trace the shape of the 2 circles onto black card and cut out. Cut fringes around the edges of the circle and curl.

4. Curl the smaller circle into the bigger one. Glue to the center of the flower. Bend the top of the floral wire and glue to the back of the flower. Prick a hole through the star and thread the wire through. Glue the star to the back of the flower covering the wire.

5. Cut out the shapes of the leaves on the green card and curl the edges. Glue the leaves to the bottom of the flower and the wire. Cover the wire with florist tape winding all the way to the bottom. The stems of the anemones are not straight so bend and twist the wire for authenticity. A bunch of anemones, tied with a ribbon makes a beautiful gift for a special friend.

8. Tissue Paper Poppies

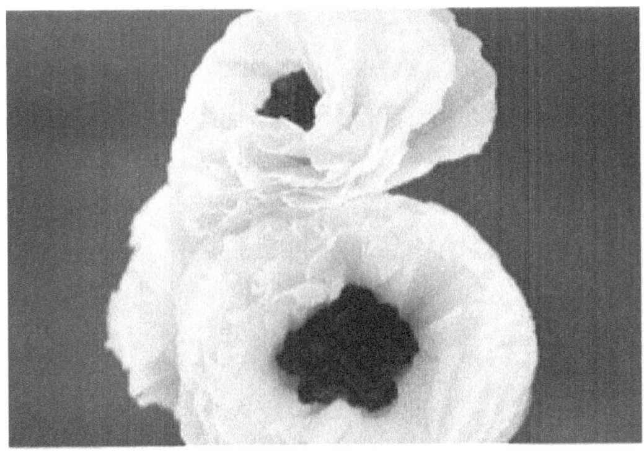

Materials

- Tissue paper
- Round lid (as per the required flower size)
- Pencil
- Scissors
- Black or brown tissue paper
- Pipe cleaners
- White craft glue

Directions

1. Place 3 pieces of tissue paper on top of one another and trace the outline of a lid. If you want a very fluffy flower, then one can add more tissue paper layers. Cut out the circle.

2. Lay 3 pieces of the brown or black tissue paper on top of one another and trace a smaller circle of about 2" in circumference. Cut out the circle.

3. Place the black circles in the center of the larger circles. Push a pipe cleaner through the center of the layers of tissue paper, leaving an inch at the top.

4. Bend over the tip of the pipe cleaner and pull the excess pipe cleaner downwards. Glue the pipe cleaner to the bottom of the flower.

5. Gently pull up the layers of tissue paper to make a beautiful poppy. Poppies are great to celebrate Memorial Day or with a little supervision, your children can make a bunch of poppies to give to their favorite teacher.

9. Tissue Paper Dahlia Gift Bags

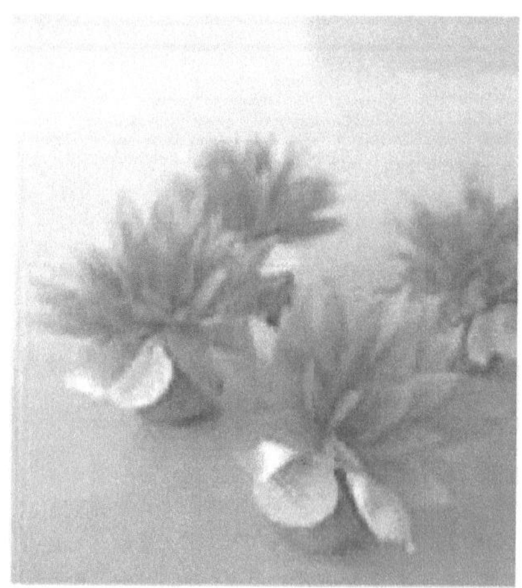

Materials

- Tissue paper
- White piece of paper
- Scissors
- Pencil
- Dahlia bulbs
- String
- Ribbon
- Card stock
- Punch

Directions

1. Take an A4 piece of paper and fold in half and again in half. 5" From the folded corner, draw the outline of 8 elongated petals. The end of the petals must end with a tip. Cut out the outline and this will be used as your template.

2. Place the template on top of folded tissue paper and trace the template. When you open the tissue paper, you will have the shape of a dahlia. Each flower will need 2 dahlia shapes. Place the 1 layer over the other, slightly overlapping the petals. Place the bulb in the center of the tissue paper and carefully draw all the tissue paper around the bulb. The petals will be at the top of the bulb.

3. Cut a piece of string and securely tie the paper together. The string must be longer than required as this will be used to tie an instruction card. Using an 8 ½" by 11" piece of paper, print the instructions on how to plant the dahlia bulb and cut out.

4. Punch a hole in the center of the card. Tie the card onto the flower with the string. Cut any excess string. Hide the string by wrapping a ribbon around the flower. Fluff up the flower. These tissue paper gift bags can also be filled with mints or sweets and used as gift bags for weddings and parties.

10. Origami Clematis Flower

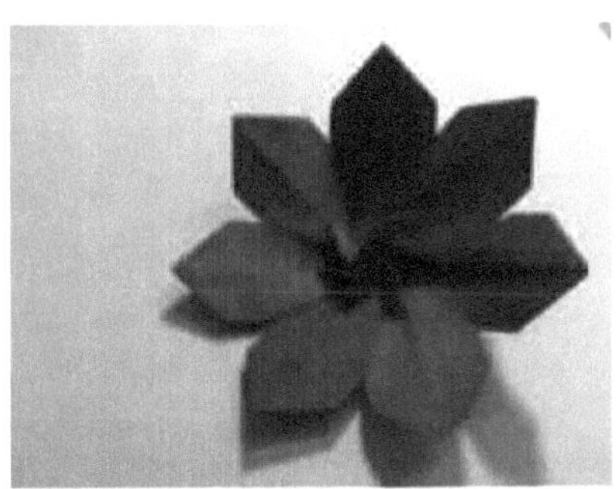

Materials

- Origami paper (2 colors)

Directions

1. Fold the color side in half and open. From the edge of the top layer fold the paper in half and crease. Turn the paper over and fold the paper to the folded edge. Fold the top two edges towards the crease (will look like an upside-down V)

2. Flip over the paper and fold the bottom right corner to the center fold and crease. Unfold. Turn the paper over and fold the left corner in the crease made above. Unfold and then reverse fold. Place the left corner on the line of the crease of the right side of the paper and fold the paper. You will now have a triangle emerging between the edges of the folded paper. Using the same directions, make a further 6 petals.

3. To connect the petals, insert the bottom corner of the petal to the next petal. Fold over the triangle to secure. Continue going round until all petals have been put in place. It may sound difficult but once you get the hang of the folding they are easy and quick to make. Your children will have lots of fun as their nimble small fingers will be able to fold the flowers with ease.

11. Double Spiraled Card Flower

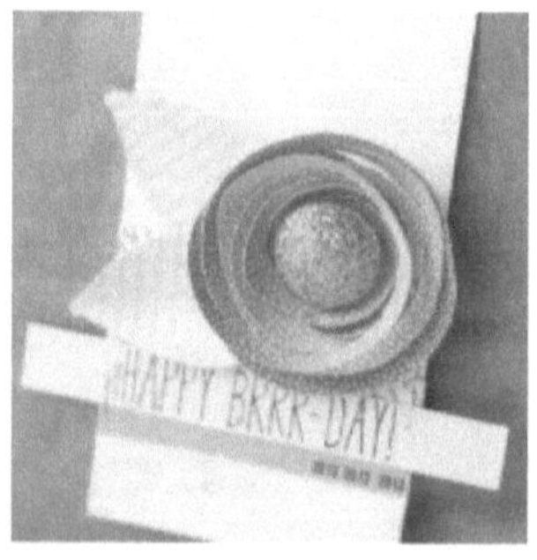

Materials

- Chart card (patterned on both sides)
- Scissors
- Tweezers
- Pencil
- Glue
- Button

Directions

1. Trace the shape of a jar lid or glass on the card. In a spiral shape, cut the circle from the outside edge towards the middle leaving a small circle in the center.

2. Take a pair of tweezers or a pencil and roll the spiral. Remove the pencil and loosen the spiral slightly so that the petals are loser. Glue the end of the spiral to the flower. Glue a button to the center. Cut out 2 leaves and attach to the bottom of the flower. Your double spiraled flower can be attached to a gift tag or can be used as an embellishment on gifts or in scrapbooking.

12. Yellow Paper Narcissus

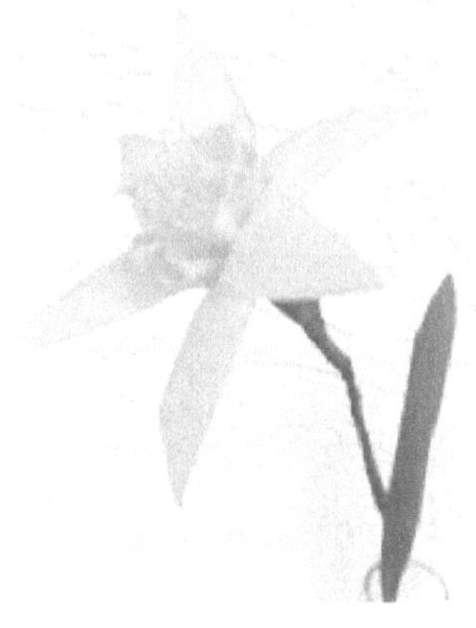

Materials

- Yellow crepe paper
- Green crepe paper
- Scissors
- Ruler
- Pencil
- Florist wire
- Craft glue
- Tall thin stemmed vase

Directions

1. Cut 3 pieces of yellow crepe paper – petals (3.5" length by 1 ½" wide). Cut 1-piece yellow crepe paper for the center stamens (1 ½" by 1 ½"). Cut 1 elongated leaf in the green crepe paper. Cut a long narrow piece of green crepe paper (to wrap around the wire).

2. Cut fringes on the paper that is reserved for the stamens. With your fingers, gently twirl each fringe. Roll up tightly and glue the ends. Take 1 of the yellow pieces for the petals and fold in half.

3. Stretch the crepe paper and wrap around the stamens and glue.

4. On the other 2 pieces of crepe paper, cut 3 x V shapes at the top. Scrunch the bottom and wrap around half the stamen. Do the same with the other piece of yellow paper.

5. Tie the bottom together with the wire. Glue the green crepe paper to the bottom of the flower and wrap around the wire including the leaf half way down the wire. Place your narcissus in a tall elongated vase.

13. Frilly Tissue Paper Flowers

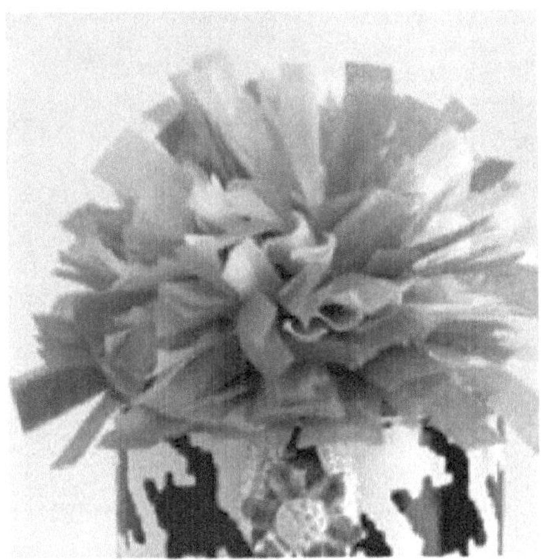

Materials

- Tissue paper
- Scissors
- Staples
- Stapler

Directions

1. Fold a piece of tissue paper in half lengthwise. Fold as many times as you want – this will determine the size of the flower. Along the length of the paper, cut every ¼".

2. Cut off the edges of the folded side – this will ensure that your flower has a frilly look. Roll up the flower and staple the bottom of the flower on both sides.

3. If you want to attach the flower to a gift, cut off the excess tissue paper underneath the staples, otherwise pop the flower on a jar or in any small vase.

14. Colorful Paper Mum Flowers

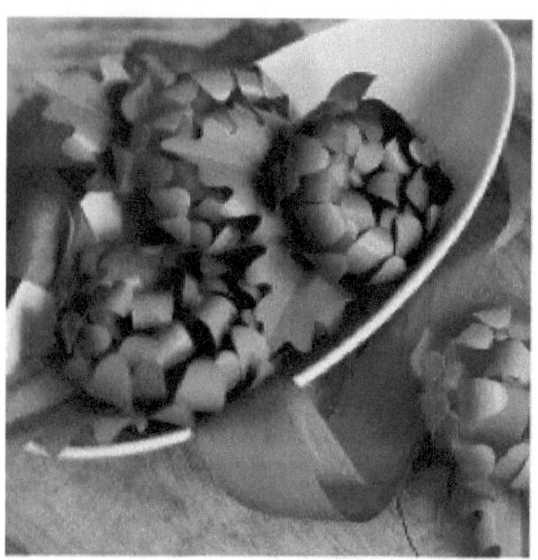

Materials

- Double sided colored paper
- Double sided green paper
- Ribbon
- Scissors
- Hot glue gun
- Flower and leaf template (if you have)
- Paper
- Pencil
- Glue

Directions

1. If you do not have a template, draw a small circle and then draw 8 elongated petals on the circle. Use this as your template for the petals. Trace 4 petals onto the colored paper and cut out. Curl the edges of the petals with a pair of scissors. Curl the center petal from the edge of the circle and each following petal a little higher up the petal.

2. Draw the shape of a leaf on the green paper and cut out. Place a spot of glue in the center of each flower and stack

together, finishing with the tightest curled flower as the center.

3. Glue the leaf to the underside of the flower. Fold a piece of ribbon to glue underneath the flower and trim. Each flower can be glued onto the lid of a storage jar or alternatively glue a clip under the flower to wear as an accessory.

15. Flower Straws with Crepe Paper

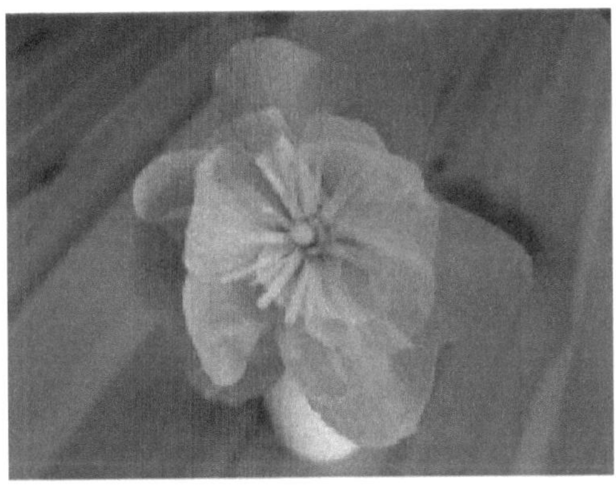

Materials

- Crepe paper streamers
- Drinking straws
- Glue
- Scissors

Directions

1. Cut crepe paper streamers into lengths of 4". At the top of the paper, cut out a wave shape which will be the top part of the petals. Dab a spot of glue on the straw and scrunch and curl the petals around the straw. Glue the end.

2. Make sure that you leave at least 1 ½" inches of the straw above the flower. Continue scrunching the rest of the petals around the straw, gluing the ends as you start each petal.

3. Cut fringes on the top of the straw and curl back with scissors. This is an easy flower for children to make and they will be occupied for hours.

16. Brown Paper Flowers

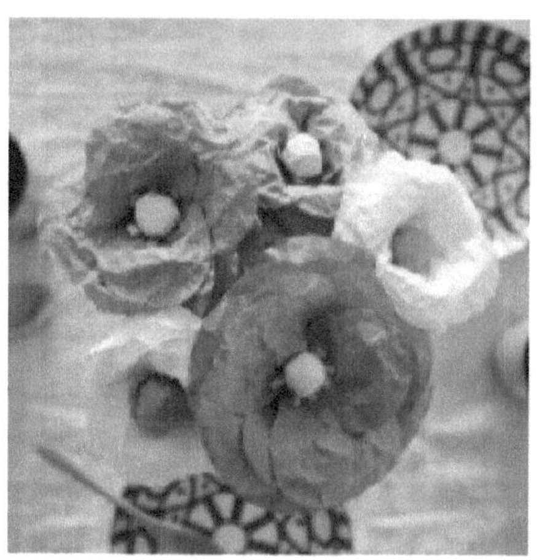

Materials

- Brown paper
- White paper
- Scraps of neon paper
- Wooden sticks (can use dowel sticks and cut to size)
- Black washi tape
- Sticky tape
- Pencil
- Ruler
- Scissors
- Tweezers

Directions

1. Take the piece of white paper and fold in half and half again. Cut out the 4 squares (you will only need 2 squares). Scrunch the 1 piece of white paper into a ball. Wrap the other piece of white paper over the ball and wrap the excess paper over the stick. Seal with sticky tape and wind the tape down the stick.

2. Cut the neon paper into 5 or 6 little strips. One by one place the neon strips around the bud and stick with sticky tape. The tweezers will help you to hold the strips in place while you stick. To make the petals, take 2 sheets of brown paper and fold lengthwise in half. Divide the width of the paper into 3 sections and draw a line across each section.

3. In each section draw a balloon shaped petal with a little tail at the end (this is what you will use to attach to the stick). Cut out the shapes (you will need 12 petals) and scrunch up the paper into a ball. Place the first petal around the bud and stick. Continue moving round until you have stuck all the petals. Cover the sticky tape with the washi tape and wind half way round the stem.

4. Starting with the bottom petals, gently bend all the petals downwards. The scrunched paper will help give you the shape of the flower. Make as many flowers as you need and pop into a vase.

17. Christmas Poinsettias

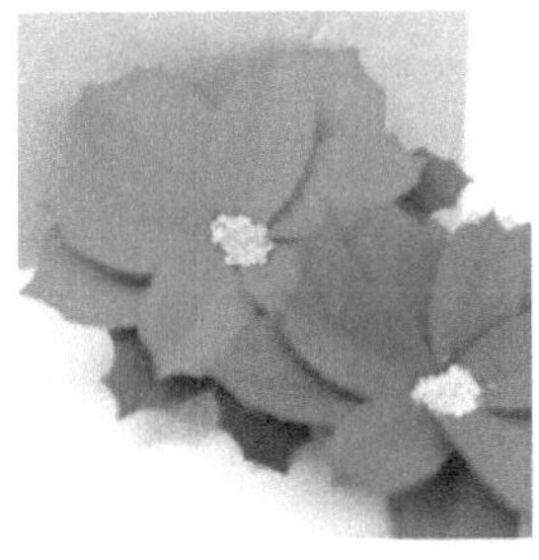

Materials

- Red card (petals)
- Green card (leaves)
- Yellow card (stamens)
- 1" Circle punch
- ½" Circle punch
- 1.75" Circle punch
- Glue
- Doily punch
- Scissors

Directions

1. Cut out ten pointed oval petals with a 2" circle punch. Fold each petal in half. On either side of the crease, cut out a small notch. Cut a small section of the bottom half of the petal straight across.

2. Punch a 1" circle. Apply a blob of glue to the center of the circle and arrange the petals around the circle.

3. Apply another blob of glue to the center of the petals and arrange the next layer of petals slightly overlapping the bottom petal.

4. Using the green card, punch ovals with the 1.75" circle punch. Create small notches around the leaves with the ½" circle punch so that the leaf looks like holly. Glue the holly leaves to the flower.

5. With a doily or similar punch create a number of tiny circles on the yellow card. Add a spot of glue to the center of the flower and sprinkle the tiny circles over the glue. These beautiful poinsettias can be used to decorate your Christmas table or as an embellishment on Christmas gifts.

18. Curled Rose Wreath

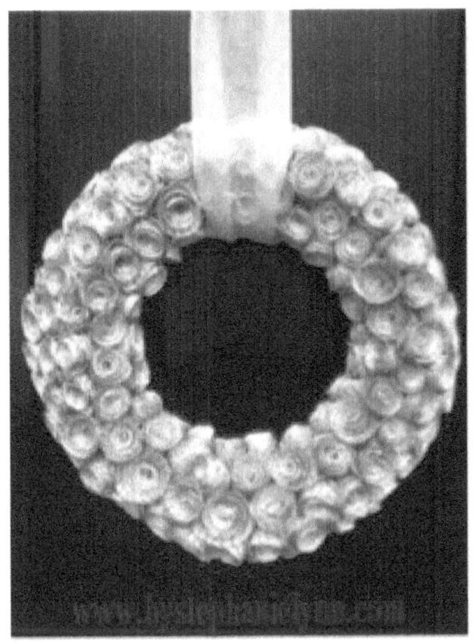

Materials

- Round foam wreath
- Pages from an old book
- Hot glue gun
- Ribbon
- Scissors
- Pencil
- Spray paint

Directions

1. Cut the pages of the book into a square. Place 3 pages on top of one another and draw a spiral circle. Cut out the spiral leaving a small circle in the center.

2. From the end of the spiral (this will become the center of the rose), start rolling the paper inwards, tightly at first and then more loosely as you get to the end.

3. Place a dab of hot glue on the back of the rose (this will hold the rose together) and place the circle at the back of the rose.

4. You will need to make a number of roses to cover the foam wreath. You can rub on an antique color ink to the edges of the rose or dip in tea – this will give the rose a more worn or older look. Spray paint the wreath in white or a light color.

5. Hot glue each rose to the wreath making sure they are as close together as possible. Cut a fairly long piece of ribbon and fold over the top of the wreath. Tie the ends of the ribbon and hang in a suitable place.

19. Pretty Origami Flowers

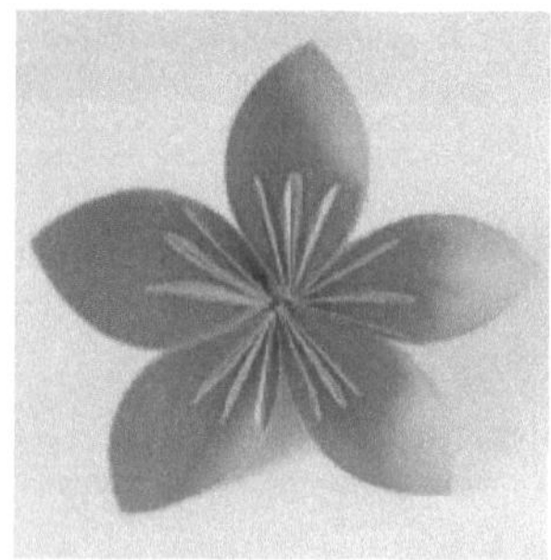

Materials

- Origami paper
- Glue

Directions

1. Flip the paper to the back side of the origami paper. Fold the origami paper from one corner to the other (you will have a triangle). Take the bottom right hand corner and fold so that the tip meets in the center.

2. Do the same with the left-hand side – you will have a smaller square. Unfold the pieces of paper back to the shape of the

triangle. With your finger open the bottom edges of the fold and press down.

3. You will now have a small triangle that sticks out from your triangle shape. Fold the point inwards towards the middle. Do the same with the left-hand side. Run a line of glue along the edge of the fold. Fold the two sides of the paper together and hold until the glue sets.

4. Make 5 petals in total for each flower. Run a line of glue on the edges of the petal and paste the next petal. Continue doing this until all 5 petals are glued together. These pretty flowers are great for table decorations.

20. Recycled Toilet Roll Holder Flowers

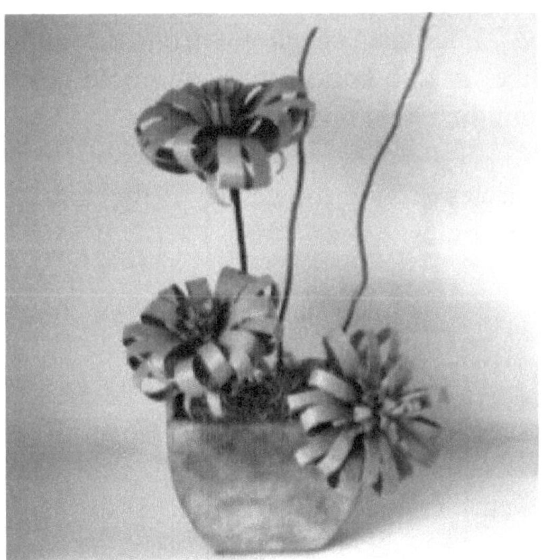

Materials

- Used toilet paper cardboard tube
- Gift wrap or paper towel cardboard tube
- Scissors
- Hot glue gun
- Skewer

- Pencil
- Brown floral tape
- Green moss
- Small pot
- Floral foam

Directions

1. Flatten the toilet roll tube in half and cut into 2 pieces.

2. Cut fringes along one side of each half. Roll the first half tightly and this will become the center of the flower. Glue the edges.

3. Roll on the second piece of toilet roll tube and glue to secure.

4. Cut at ½" intervals, 16 circles from the gift wrap or paper towel tube. At the bottom of each circle cut out a V shape. Do not cut the circle open.

5. Glue 8 circles around the center of the flower and then glue the next 8 circles.

6. Push the skewer in at the bottom of the flower to form the stem.

7. Cut a piece of cardboard tubing 3" by 4" and cut 1-inch elongated petals with a pointed tip. Roll each tip around a pencil to curl. Glue to the bottom layer of the flower.

8. Wrap the floral tape around the base of the flower and down the skewer. Make as many flowers as you would need for the flower pot.

9. Cut floral foam to fit the size of the pot. Cover with moss. Cut the flowers at different lengths and arrange in the flower pot.

21. Flower Garland Made with Paper Napkins

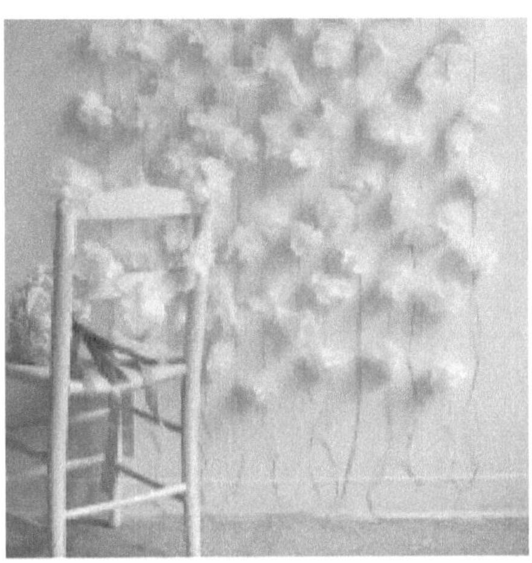

Materials

- Cocktail paper napkins
- Reinforcement labels
- Scissors
- Ribbon
- Pencil
- Ruler
- Wooden dowel or metal rod
- Washi tape in the color of the flowers
- Hooks

Directions

1. Fold a cocktail paper napkin in a triangle and fold again twice. Draw a petal shape on the open edge of the napkin leaving the folded edge attached. Cut out the shape.

2. Unfold all the layers and place on top of one another. Each layer must be slightly apart so that the petals alternate to have a flower shape).

3. Fold upwards from the center (underneath the petal layer). Twist the center firmly in order to hold all the flowers together. Open and fluff all the petals. Make as many flowers as required.

4. Cut 13 strands of ribbon, each 6 feet long. Attach the first flower to the ribbon with the reinforcement label. Measure 7 inches and attach another reinforcement label.

5. Wrap over the ribbon and secure to another flower. Wind washi tape to the length of the wooden dowel or metal rod. Tie each garland onto the metal rod or wooden dowel. Drill 2 holes into the wall and attach the rod to the hooks.

22. Crepe Paper Bubble Flowers

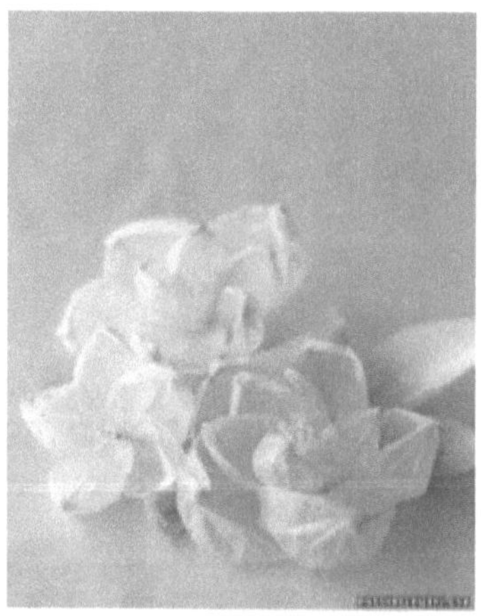

Materials

- Artificial stamens
- Crepe paper
- 24 Gauge floral wire
- Floral tape
- 1 ½" Styrofoam ball
- Scissors

Directions

1. Cut 5 pieces of crepe paper 4" by 2 ¼" - this will become the petals. Wrap one piece of crepe paper around the Styrofoam ball. Twirl either end of the crepe paper and remove from the ball. Continue this process until you have shaped all 5 petals. Put the stamens and 1 petal on the floral wire and attach with floral tape.

2. Place the next petal and attach. As you attach the balance of the flowers, slightly overlap them with the next petal. Wind the floral tape around the rest of the floral wire.

3. Cut off the pointy tips of each flower and gently pull the petals away from the center. The crepe paper bubble flowers are a great addition to gift packages or can be used as decoration.

23. Dogwood Paper Flowers

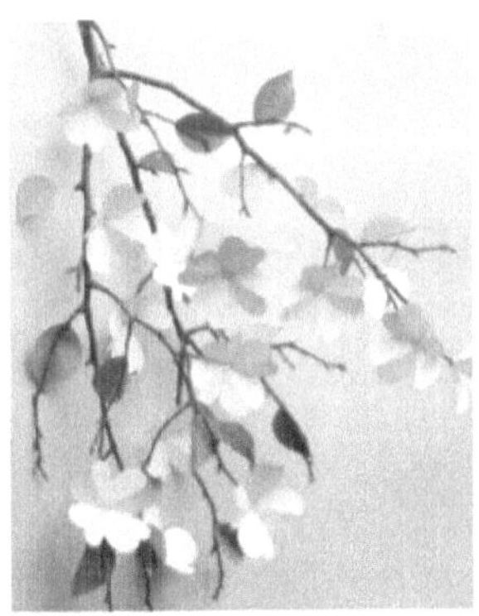

Materials

- White and green card stock
- Dogwood petal template
- Scissors
- New eraser
- Ruler

- Starburst stamp
- Green ink
- Clear craft glue
- Thin branches

Directions

1. Cut 5" squares from the white chart card. Fold the square in half and in half again. Open the square and now fold diagonally twice. Fold the square back into the originally folded shape. If you have a dogwood petal template then trace onto the square. If not, draw a rounded heart shape onto the crepe paper. The bottom of the heart will be at the fold.

2. Cut out the outline of the shape. Snip a tiny piece off the bottom of the folded area. Open up the flower shape. Dip the side of the eraser into the green ink and press gently along the folds of the petals. Stamp the starburst shape into the center of the petal. Cut out the shape of a leaf in the green card stock. Glue the petals and leaves to the branches. Display your spring blossoms as a centerpiece on your dining room table.

24. Long Stemmed Valentine Roses

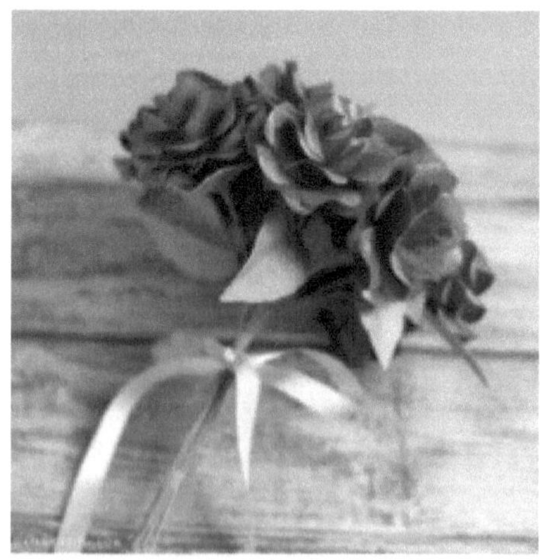

Materials

- Printed copies of roses and leaves (both sides of page)
- Scissors
- Hot glue gun
- Florist wire
- Florist tape
- Ribbon

Directions

1. Cut out the shape of seven petal pieces (3 single petals; 1x3 petals; 1x4 petals; 2x5 petals) and one leaf for each rose. Curl the corner edges of each petal.

2. Fold the leaf along the spine. Curl the edges of the leaf. Using hot glue, form cones with the 3, 4 and 5 petal shapes. Fold back one inch of the florist wire. Glue the edge of one petal to the florist wire and roll, leaving one of the curled edges.

3. Add a drop of glue to the bottom of the next single petal and wrap around the first petal. Re-curl the edges. Add the third single petal as above. Push the wire through the rest of your petals starting with the 3 petals, then 4 and then 5 petals.

4. Each time add a drop of glue and paste onto the petals above. Move the petals around so that it looks like a rose. Beginning at the base of the rose; wind florist tape around the wire, gently stretching as you go.

5. Attach a leaf at an appropriate place and continue wrapping the florist tape until you have reached the end of the wire. At the base of the leaf place a drop of glue and hold securely until dry. Repeat the process and make as many roses as you would need. Hold the roses together and tie with ribbon.

25. Mother's Day Bouquet

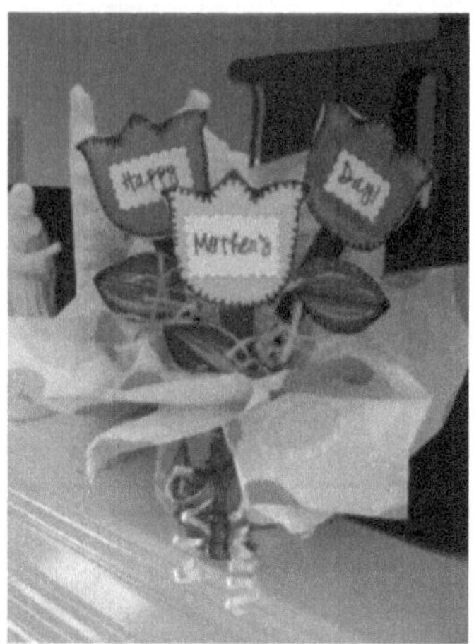

Materials

- Tissue paper
- Tin can
- Scissors
- Photo stickers
- Chart card
- Green paint
- Paint brush
- Jumbo craft sticks
- Ribbon
- Green Easter grass
- Clip art flowers and leaves
- Colored pens
- Glue

Directions

1. Paint the crafts sticks green and leave to dry. Download flower shapes and leaves from clip art and paste the shapes on the chart card. Color in the flowers and leaves.

2. Print a message for each flower. For example, "I love you" or "Happy Mother's Day". Cut out the shapes. Attach a craft stick to each flower with the photo stickers or glue.

3. Glue on a leaf to each stick. Fill the can with Easter grass. Arrange the flowers in the can. Cut a piece of tissue paper in half and place the can in the middle of the paper.

4. Gather the paper around the can and secure with a ribbon. Cut a few strands of ribbon and tie around the can. Curl the ribbon. Your kids will have a lot of fun making their very own bouquet for Mother's Day.

26. Daffodils Using Egg Cartons

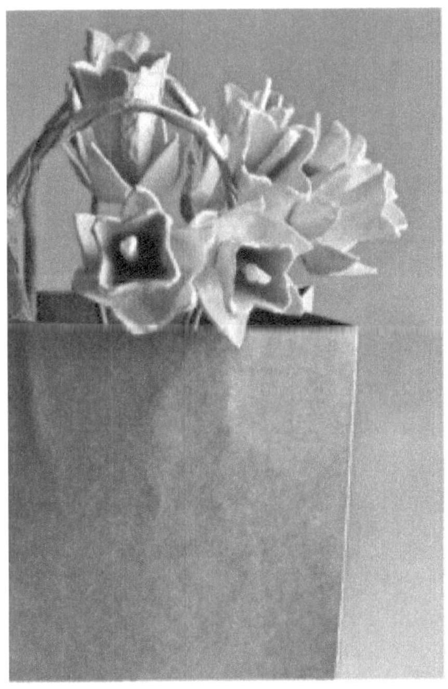

Materials

- Paper egg cartons (two different sizes)
- Pipe cleaners

- Florist tape
- Yellow crepe paper
- Utility knife
- Scissors (curved blade)
- Yellow acrylic paint
- Vase (optional)
- Floral foam (optional)
- Gift bag

Directions

1. Remove the shapes from the egg cartons. Divide the egg cup into 6 equal sections and draw in the shape of the petals so that they are equal in size. Cut out the shapes.

2. Using the triangle shape of the egg carton cut out the shape and cut small V's at the top (this will be used for the inside of the daffodil).

3. Paint the egg carton shapes in yellow paint. Add white glue to the inside of the cup as well as the bottom of the inside cup and glue together. At the center of the cup, make a hole.

4. Gently wrap florist tape around the pipe cleaner. Cut a 2" x 2" piece of yellow crepe paper.

5. At the end of the stem, put on some glue and wrap the tissue paper around the pipe cleaner (this will create the stamen).

6. Push your stem through the top of the flower and pull through so that the green side is below.

7. Using the above method, make as many daffodils as you need. Put the flowers into a vase and place into the gift bag or you can put the flowers into floral foam and place inside the gift bag.

27. Potted Paper Tulips

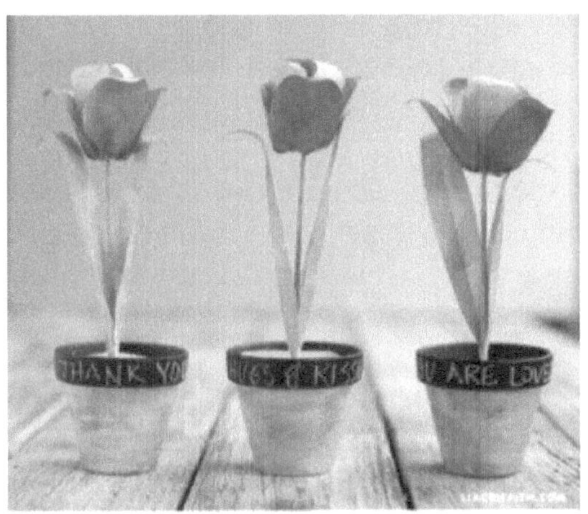

Materials

- Paper
- Watercolor paints
- Brush
- Scissors
- Florist wire
- Skewer
- Hot glue
- Florist foam
- Small pot

Directions

1. Draw 6 oval and 1 round shapes onto the paper and paint in two different colors (red/pink for the petals). Draw 1 rectangle shape and paint in a deeper shade of red (stamen).

2. Draw 1 long rectangle shape and paint green (stem). Draw 2 long oval shapes pond paint in green (leaves).

3. Cut the skewer to the height required and wind the green strip of paper over the skewer. Glue on either side to secure the paper. Cut fringes onto the rectangle shape (stamen). Punch a small hole in the round shape and slip onto the skewer.

4. Glue on the fringe (stamen). Cut small slits at the base of the petals and curl the upper edges. Glue petals under the circle – the same colors inside (petals curving inwards). Glue the same color petals on the outside (petals curving outwards).

5. Glue the leaves to the stem. Cut the floral foam to fit into the pot and cover the top with paper that is painted in the same color green as the leaves. Place the skewer into the pot. You can make 2 or 3 pots of daffodils and place on a windowsill.

28. Origami Peach Blossoms

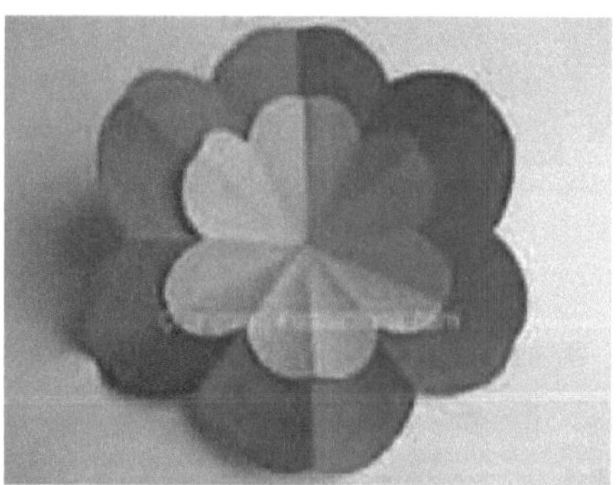

Materials

- 6" x 6" Origami paper
- Smaller square piece origami paper (different color)
- Scissors

Directions

1. With the color side down, fold the paper in half on the horizontal axis. Fold paper in half on the vertical axis, crease

well and unfold. Fold the right-hand edge towards the top point and crease the side edge only. Fold the paper from the new creased edge and fold up towards the top and crease the edge.

2. From this creased edge, fold once again to the top and crease. From the middle crease fold the paper inwards and crease well. Fold the lower left-hand edge and fold over. Crease well. Fold the entire right-hand side paper over and firmly crease. Cut along the curved line.

3. Discard the upper portion and unfold the paper. You will now have created a large origami blossom. Take a smaller square piece of paper and fold in the same manner as above. Place the smaller blossom inside the larger blossom and you will now have a beautiful peach blossom.

29. Paper Flowers with Flair

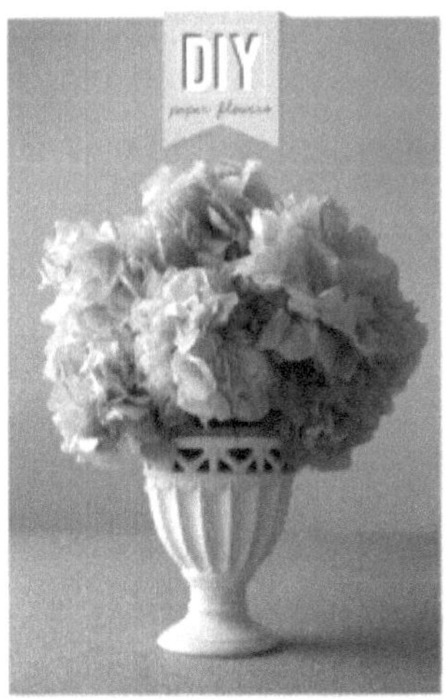

Materials

- Yellowed sewing patterns
- Ruler
- Scissors

* 24 Gauge floral wire
* Skewers (optional)
* Vase (optional)

Directions

1. Place 10 sheets of yellowed sewing patterns on top of one another. Measure a 10" square and cut. Fold the paper in 1" folds in an accordion fashion. Pinch in the middle of the folded paper and tie together with the floral wire. Cut both edges in a round shape.

2. Unfold the paper carefully and fan out into a large flower. Scrunch the paper gently and it will look like a hydrangea. Cut floral foam and place into a vase.

3. Wrap the remaining wire around a skewer and push into the floral foam. You will now have a spectacular vase of flowers that can be used as a center piece decoration for any party or festive event.

30. Origami Hyacinth

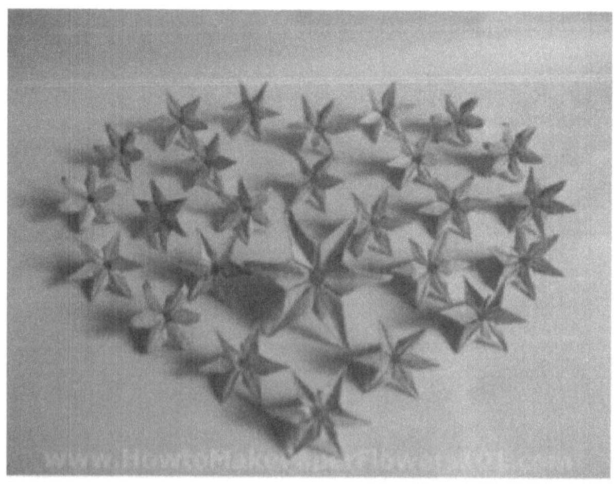

Materials

- Cardboard
- Compass
- Pencil
- Scissors
- Origami paper

Directions

1. To make an equilateral hexagon, draw a circle onto the card with the compass. Divide the circle in to 6 equal parts and mark. Join the marked points of the circle with a ruler and you will end up with 6 straight lines.

2. Cut along the lines and you will have the shape of the equilateral hexagon. Use this as your pattern. Trace the shape onto the origami paper. Fold the paper along the vertical axis and crease well.

3. Do the same with all the other points. Turn the paper the other way round and fold in the shape of an envelope.

4. Fold the paper from the bottom to the center and crease well. Do this on both sides. From the center of all the folds, bring the folded sections to the center. It will look like a starfish.

5. Fold the paper together and you will be left with one piece facing the top. Open the section and fold so that it is open. Continue to do with each section until you have a rectangular shape – the tip at the bottom and triangle at the top.

6. Fold over the top pieces into a smaller triangle and crease. Open these folded pieces to the outside. Fold the top of each edge to the center. Gently pull open and you will have the shape of one hyacinth blossom.

31. Paper Flower to Decorate Cupcakes

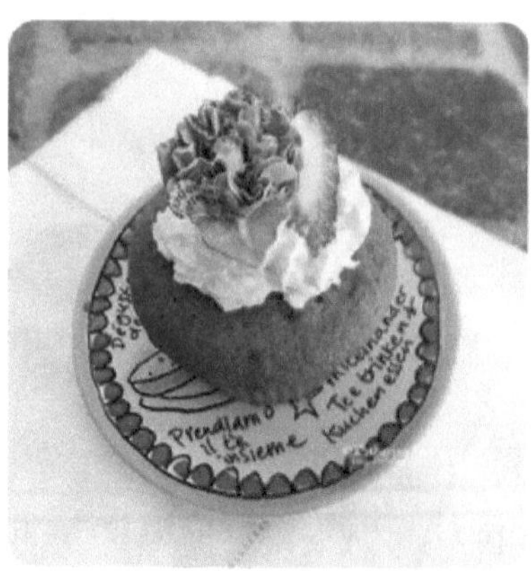

Materials

- Die cut flower shapes (different types of paper and sizes)
- Brad (paper fastener)
- Water
- Toothpick
- Glue
- Liquid pearls
- Die cut leaves

Directions

1. Layer together 2 to 4 pieces (each size) of the die cut flowers.
   Use a mix of different colored papers. Secure the papers with
   a brad or paper fastener. Wet each layer of paper with water
   and shape into a bud. Unfold the paper and remove the brad.
   Put a drop of glue on the toothpick and push through the hole
   left by the brad. Add a large drop of liquid pearl in the center
   of the bud.

2. Using the die cut leaves, wet with water and gently push the
   leaves together. Attach with glue to the bottom of the flower.
   Once dry place in a cupcake.

32. Colored Paper Spider Mums

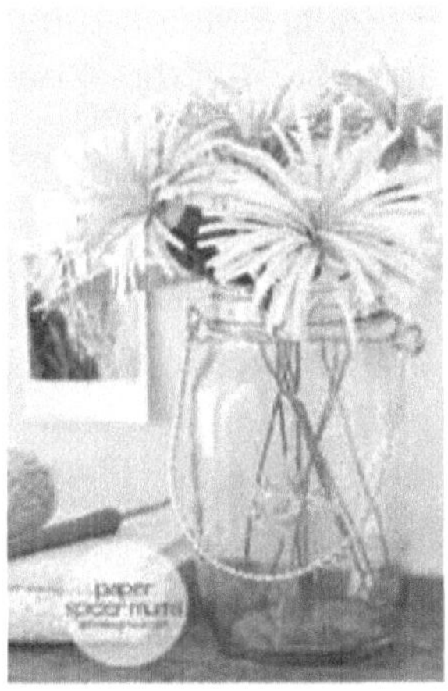

Materials

- 12" x 12" Card paper in different colors
- Fringe scissors (or large cutting scissors)
- Scotch tape
- Floral wire stems
- Green floral tape
- Glue or hot glue gun
- Tissue paper
- Mason jar or container

Directions

1. Cut the paper into 2" to 3" wide strips or to the size of flower you want. Cut the paper with the fringe scissors or cut fringes into the paper.

2. Roll up the paper to form a bud and tape the bud closed. Place the floral wire through the bud and glue at the bottom. Put a small piece of tissue paper between mums the bud and the wire stem (this will balance the difference in size). Wrap the bud and stem with floral tape.

3. Pull the paper fringes outwards and curve slightly with your thumb or gently with a pair of scissors. You are not going to curl the paper but you are rather going to curve the fringes so that they flow outwards. Pop the flowers into a mason jar and display.

33. Ice Cream Cone Flower Bouquets

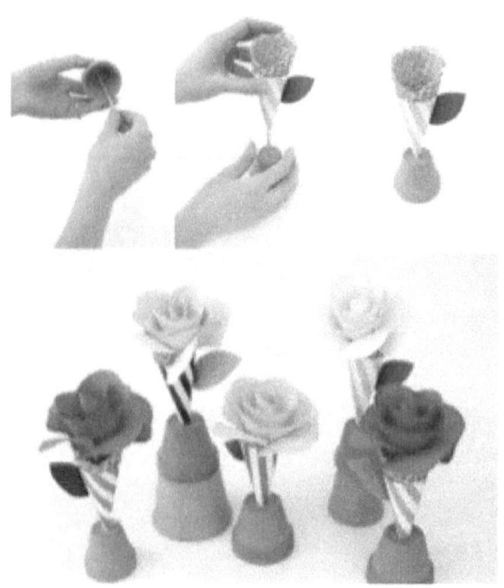

Materials

- Ice cream cones (waffle or sugar)
- X-Acto knife
- Glue gun
- Cutting board
- Scissors
- Skewers
- Garden pot 2" (to use as a stand)
- Brightly colored paper (flowers)
- Green paper (leaves)
- Striped paper
- Double sided tape
- Party hat

Directions

1. Trace the shape of a party hat and reduce to size to cover the cone. Trace the shape onto the striped paper. Cut out the template and secure around the cone with double sided tape. Draw a lemon shape (2" wide x 1 ½" height) onto a piece of paper (to make the petals).

2. Trace onto the colored paper and cut out 11 petals. For the center of the rose, make a tube shape and glue the end together. Squeeze the next petal and glue onto the bud. Continue with this method until you have used 5 petals – each petal must be looser as you go along.

3. With a pencil curl the remaining 4 petals at the top and glue the bottom to the other petals. Cut the skewers to a length of 3-4". Glue the skewer to the center of the bud and hold to dry firmly. Cut out leaves on the green paper and place a drop of glue on the top of the leaf and attach to the cone.

4. Insert another small piece of skewer and insert into the hole of the pot. Insert the bottom of the skewer into the cone. This is a great gift to cheer up a friend or use them at birthday parties.

34. Pencils Decorated with Paper Flowers

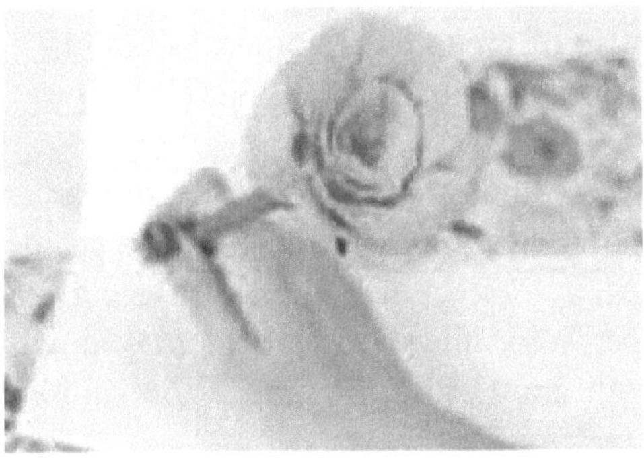

Materials

- Crepe paper in 3 colors (center, petals and leaves)
- Pencil or pen
- Floral tape
- Craft glue
- Scissors
- Lollipop stick or skewer

Directions

1. Cut a 2" x 1" strip of crepe paper as well as a small square for the center of the flower. Cover the eraser of the pencil or the lid of a pen with the square and secure with floral tape.

2. Cut a fringe on the one side of the crepe paper and wrap around the pencil and secure with floral tape. Cut 5 small crepe paper petal shapes and 6 larger petal shapes. Stretch the center of each petal with your thumb and curl the top of the petal with a skewer.

3. Using the small petals, wrap each one around the pencil rotating as you go so that the petals spread out. Secure with floral tape.

4. Add the larger petals securing each time with floral tape. Each petal should overlap the opening of the last petal. Cut a 1" x 3" strip of green crepe paper, folding in half and again in half. Cut both ends to make a point.

5. Wrap this around the base of the flower and secure with floral tape continuing to wrap the tape to the bottom of the pencil. Cut a 1" strip of crepe and place a dot of glue on the floral tape. Wind the crepe all the way down the pencil and secure with another dot of glue. Who said that writing can't be fun?

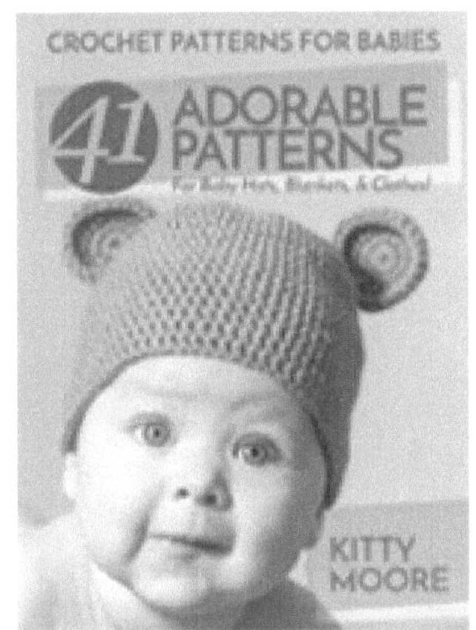

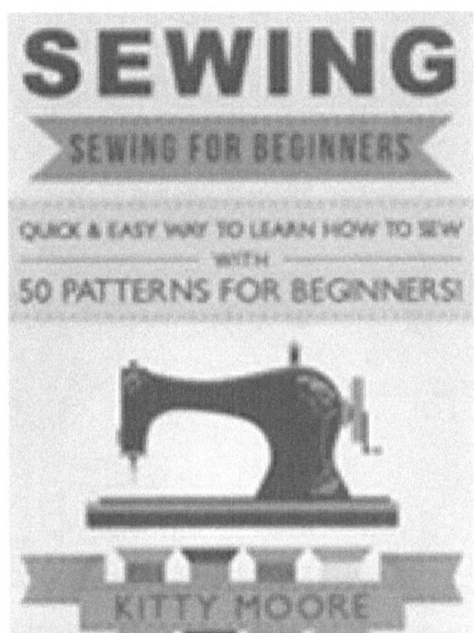

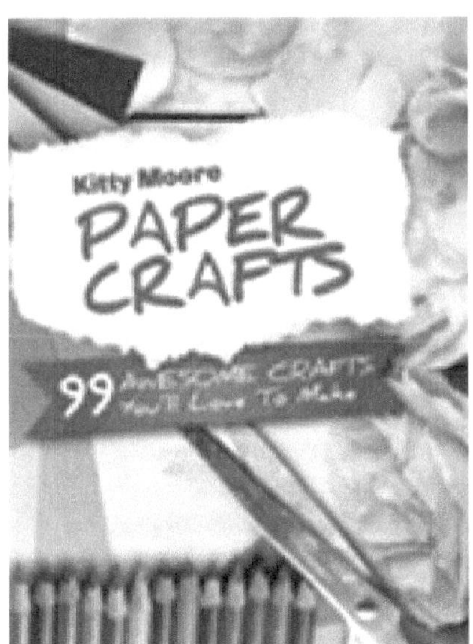

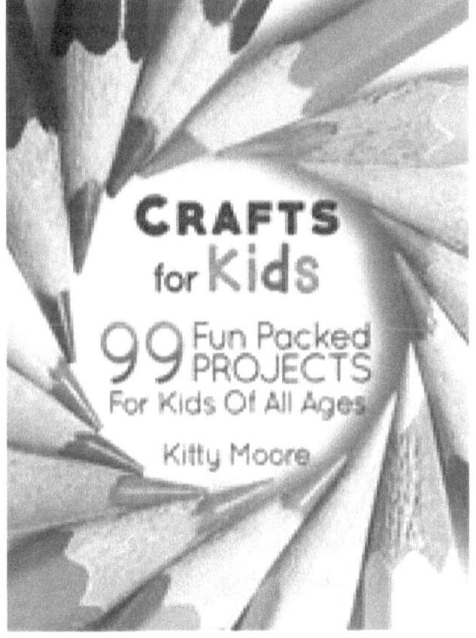

Check out Kitty's books at:

ArtsCraftsAndMore.com/go/books

35. Creative Lisianthus Flowers with Tissue Paper

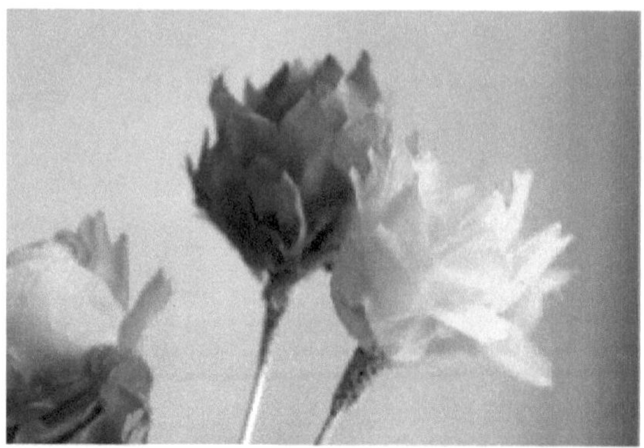

Materials

- Tissue paper
- Scissors
- Wooden skewer
- Glue
- Washi tape

Directions

1. Remove all the tissue paper from the pack and do not separate. Mark the tissue paper every 4" and cut through all the layers.

2. Start folding the tissue paper every 0.6" and crease very well after each fold. At the top of the paper cut out a V shape. Open up the folded strip and you will see a zig zag pattern.

3. Glue the skewer to the lower half of the tissue paper and gently wrap the paper around the stick. Scrunch the paper as you roll so that the flower can open. Roll a little further down the skewer so that the center of the flower is visible.

4. After you have wound all the paper, secure the flower with washi tape. Separate each petal, fluffing them out to add more volume to the flower. These flowers can be a beautiful decoration or combined with other flowers to form a bouquet.

36. Beautiful Tissue Paper Peonies

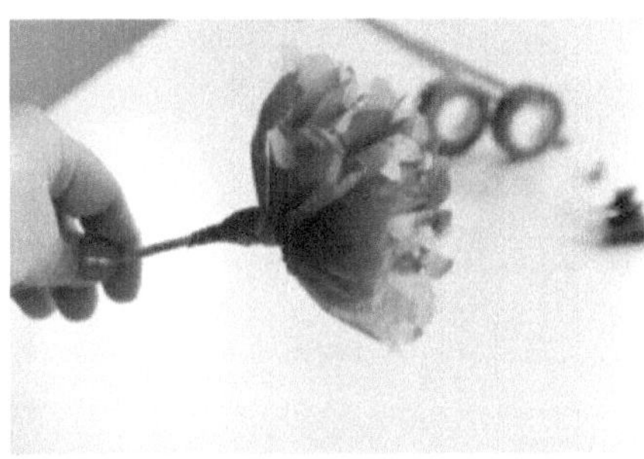

Materials

- Pack of tissue paper
- Scissors
- Glue
- Wooden skewer
- Washi or scotch tape
- Floral foam
- Vase

Directions

1. Cut the pack of tissue paper into a strip of 4" long. Unfold the strip and start pleating the strip in 0.4" widths. Each time you fold make sure to crease well. One peony will have in the region of 6 to 8 pleats. Cut at the required length. To create a curved petal look, cut the top in an upside U.

2. Place the skewer at the edge of the tissue paper and dot with glue. Still pleated, wrap the tissue paper around the stick and secure with washi or scotch tape at the end.

3. Open the folds to the left and right of the skewer until the flower is nicely fluffed out. Cut the floral form to fit a vase and insert. Push and arrange the skewers into the foam. If the sticks are too long, cut shorter so that you have a ball like effect in the vase.

37. Perfect Paper Dahlias

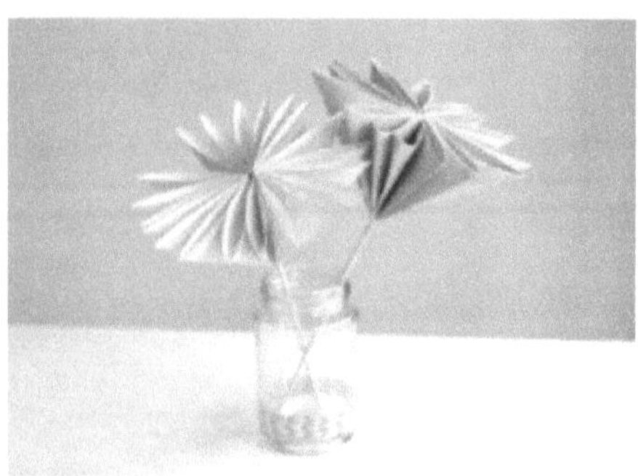

Materials

- 2 Square pieces of paper (if possible different color or design on either side)
- Craft glue
- Wooden skewer

Directions

1. Purchase paper that is 6" x 6" or cut to size. If you don't find paper that has different colors or patterns on either side, then glue two pieces of paper together. Diagonally join the bottom left hand corner to the top right hand corner (you should have the shape of a triangle). Crease well.

2. Unfold and do the same with the other two corners. Make sure that you crease well. Turn the paper over to the other side. Fold the bottom section to the top section horizontally. Crease well. Open the paper and this time fold the left edge towards the right edge vertically. Crease well. Unfold the

paper and you will see an X shape being made by the creased lines. Fold in the papers on either side of the X so that you have a thin X shape to the paper. Fold all the sections to one side.

3. Open the paper and run a strip of glue along the central line and push all the edges towards the glued section. Hold firmly until all the sections are secured. Gently open the petals with your fingers. Using the same process, make another 3 or 4 flowers. Position each flower next to the skewer and glue the narrow part of the paper to the stick. Hold firmly until all the petals are secure. Flip the petals right side up and you will have a beautiful dahlia.

38. Tissue Paper Pompoms

Tissue Paper Pom Poms

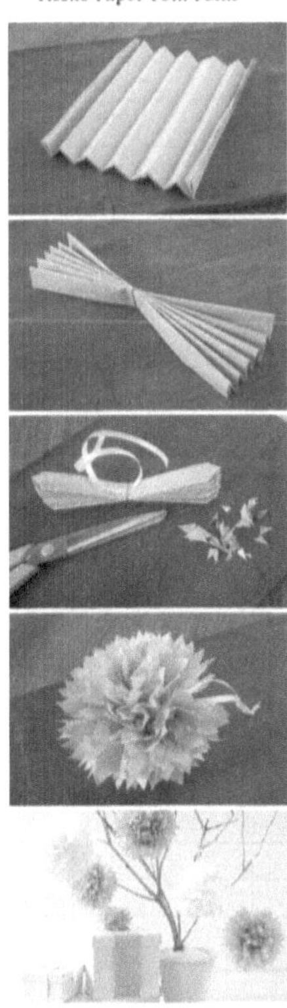

Materials

- Pack of tissue paper
- Florist wire
- Ribbon
- Scissors

Directions

1. You will need to use the full pack of tissue paper – do not separate the pieces. Depending on how large you would like the pompoms, cut the width of the paper accordingly.

2. Fold the tissue paper at 1" intervals, accordion style. Have approximately 6 folds. Join at the middle with florist wire and cut when secured. Cut the edges on both sides in different sized V shapes.

3. Place a piece of ribbon through the florist wire. Open the tissue paper on either side until you have a pompom shape. Tie the pompoms as decorations to your Christmas tree or use as any other party decoration.

39. Antique Rose Paper Flowers

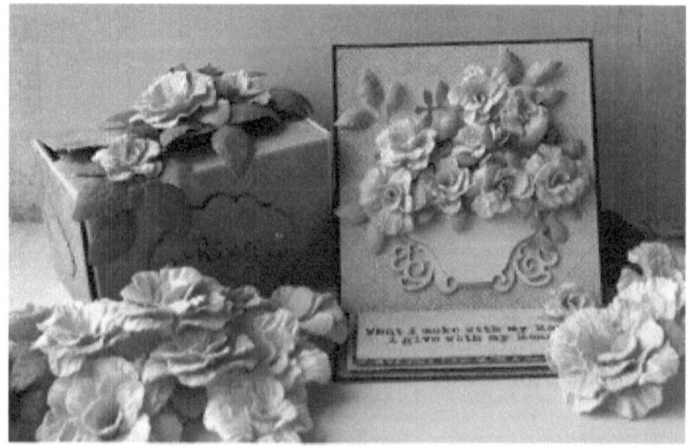

Materials

- Die cut 5 petal flowers (hand-made paper)
- Die cut leaves
- Water spray
- Cutting mat
- Stylus
- Heat tool
- Glue
- Tweezers

Directions

1. Cut some of the flowers into separate petals. Lightly spray the petals with water.

2. Wrap a petal around a stylus. Gently pinch the ends of the petals together. Dry with a heating tool.

3. Place a whole petal through the point of the stylus. Put a spot of glue on the inside of the petal and start gluing the petals together, arranging in the shape of a flower. Hold each petal for a few seconds to make sure the glue is dry.

4. Take a single petal and fold over. Hold with a tweezer, add a spot of glue and stick to the center of the flower. You may have to add a few single petals to the middle of the flower. Cut off the bubble of glue at the back of the flower.

5. Take the die cut leaves, lightly spray with water and wind over the stylus. Pinch the sides together.

6. Cut off the bottom edge of the leaf and holding with a tweezer, glue to the bottom of the flower. These are great flowers to use for cards, decoration on gifts or picture frames.

40. Fluffy 3D Dahlias

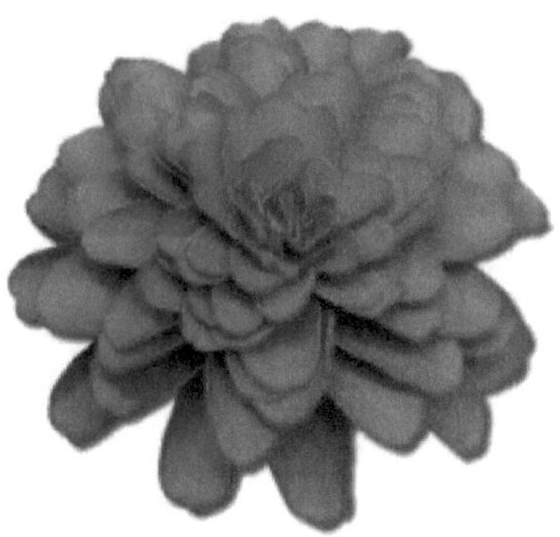

Materials

- Set of different size petals
- Skewer
- Glue
- Ink

Directions

1. Cut and sort out your petals according to the different sizes. Place the skewer on the side of the petal and gently curve upwards around the skewer.

2. Starting with like size petals, dot the middle with glue and paste together. Stagger the petals so that they overlap the petals of the one below. Continue with this process until all the same size petals have been glued. Leave the smaller petals until the end.

3. To start stacking the petals, use the largest size at the bottom, and layer upwards with the smaller sizes. As you glue each segment, press firmly in the middle to ensure that the glue adheres.

4. For the center petal, take a small petal and squash together and then glue the other smaller petals around.

5. Glue to the main flower and hold down with a skewer to dry. Dip the skewer into ink and dab around the edges. The dahlia can be made in a variety of sizes and the smaller ones are great to use for special occasion cards and in scrapbooking.

41. Glitter Glue Accordion Flowers

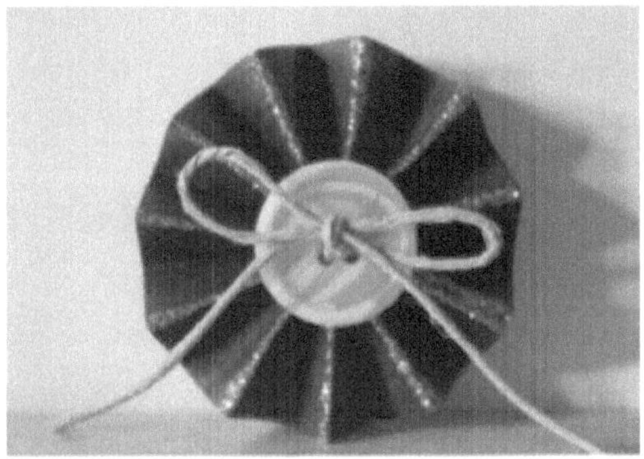

Materials

- Thick double-sided paper
- Scotch tape
- Quick drying glue
- Glue pen
- Glitter
- Embellishments such as: buttons, crystals, bows etc.

Directions

1. Cut the paper into 1" by 12" strips. Score the card every ½". Start folding the card in an accordion style. Join the two edges together and stick with a piece of scotch tape.

2. Gently push all the edges from the outside towards the center, so that it makes a circle. Place a small amount of

quick drying glue in the center and hold firmly together until dry.

3. On the raised areas of the flower, run a line of glue. Sprinkle glitter over the glue and wait to dry. Shake off the excess glitter and now you can embellish the center. Paste on a button or crystal or make a ribbon bow. This is really a fun and easy activity to do with your children.

42. Scalloped Paper Flowers

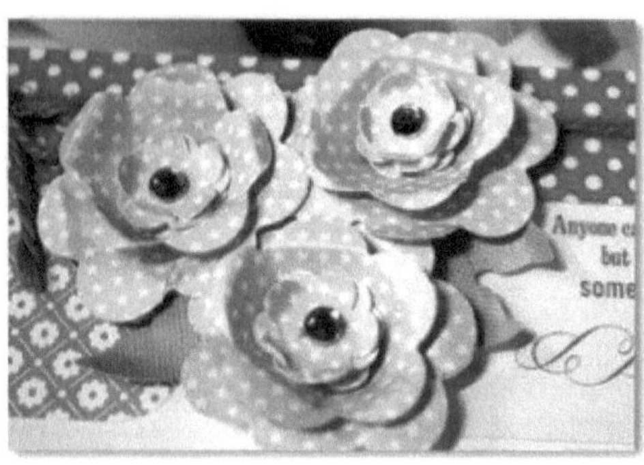

Materials

- Scallop circle maker
- Friendship micro maker
- Craft paper
- Small pieces foam
- Scissors
- Glue
- Colored bead

Directions

1. Punch 3 circles with the scallop circle maker. Cut out one scallop and on the other cut out two scallops. Fold and join the cut scallops with a little glue.

2. Place a drop of glue in the center of the largest scallop and attach the next size until all three scallops have been glued together. Cut 3 small flowers with the friendship micro maker.

3. Attach a small piece of foam in the center of the scallops and glue on a small flower. Repeat with the process with the other two flowers. Paste a colored bead in the center of the flower. These scalloped flowers are perfect as part of a gift decoration.

43. Embossed Foil Flower

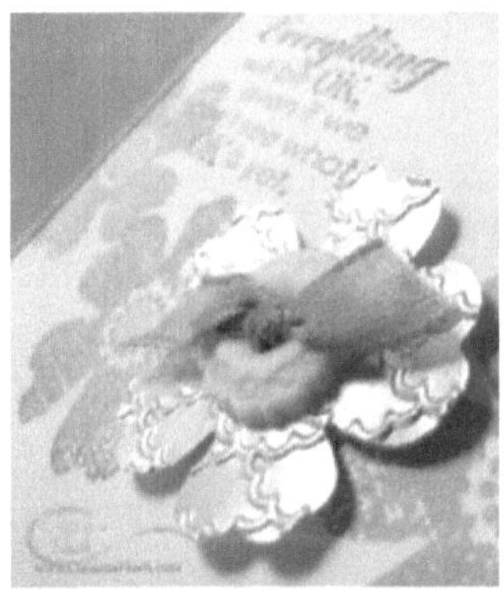

Materials

- Embossed foil
- Button
- Ribbon
- Glue
- Scissors
- Tracing paper
- Maker

Directions

1. Trace the shape of a flower – the size of flower depending on your requirements. Trace the pattern on the underside of the

embossed foil sheet. Cut out the shape. Thread a piece of ribbon through the button holes and tie in a bow.

2. Glue a button to the center of the flower. These embossed flowers give that extra sparkle to your craft projects.

44. Bright and Sunny Paper Daisies

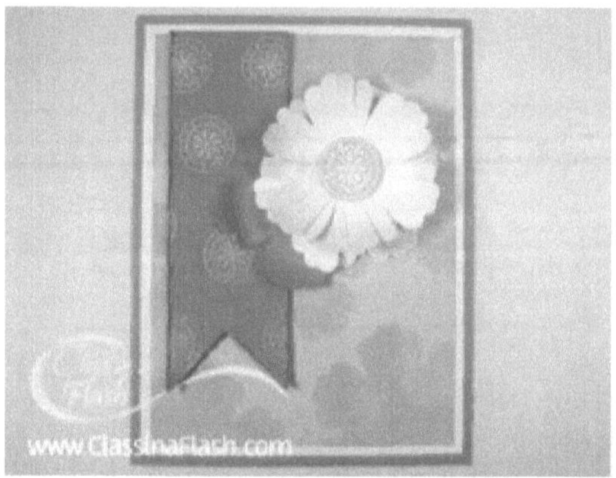

Materials

- Scallop circle maker
- Paper
- Scissors
- Fringe scissors
- Knife
- Glue
- Button

Directions

1. Cut out as many petals as you need with the scallop maker. Cut the edges of the petals with fringe scissors or make your own fringes with scissors.

2. With a knife, twirl the edges from the under-side of the petals. Glue a button in the center. The daisies can be made

in a variety of sizes and colors. They are a perfect embellishment to get-well cards.

45. Colorful Tissue Paper Flowers

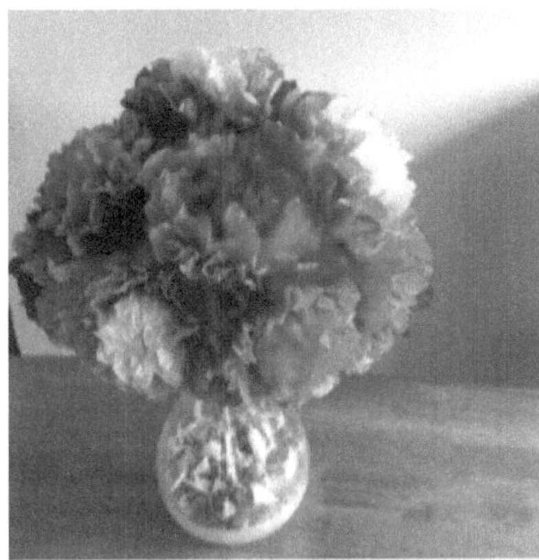

Materials

- 12 Sheets of tissue paper (3 colors)
- 12 Pipe cleaners or flexible wire
- Scissors
- Vase
- Ribbon
- Double sided tape

Directions

1. Unfold the tissue paper and lay three colors on top on one another. Place the tissue paper in front of you and fold over in 1" intervals. Flip over and once again fold over in 1" intervals. Fold the paper so that it is in the shape of an accordion.

2. Fold the paper in half and secure with a pipe cleaner. Do not scrunch the paper when you do this. The balance of the pipe cleaner will serve as the stem.

3. Fold both sides of the paper in half towards the middle pipe cleaner but facing the other way. Fold the pipe cleaner in the fold. Cut the paper in 3 equal sizes ensuring that the pipe cleaner remains in the center of each piece.

4. Trim both edges in a circular shape. Keep the off-cuts as you will use them later for the bottom of the vase. Hold the pipe cleaner just underneath the paper and gently open up the tissue paper segments. Start with the top layer and pull upwards. Pull the second layer towards the top layer.

5. Pull the bottom layer to the bottom. Turn the flower upside down and gently push the bottom paper upwards towards the middle layer. Place the tissue paper off-cuts at the bottom of the vase.

6. Bend the pipe cleaners slightly and start arranging the flowers in the vase. You almost want the flowers to have a pompom look in the vase. Cut a piece of ribbon the circumference of the vase. Place around the vase and join together with double side tape.

46. Easy Crepe Paper Red Roses

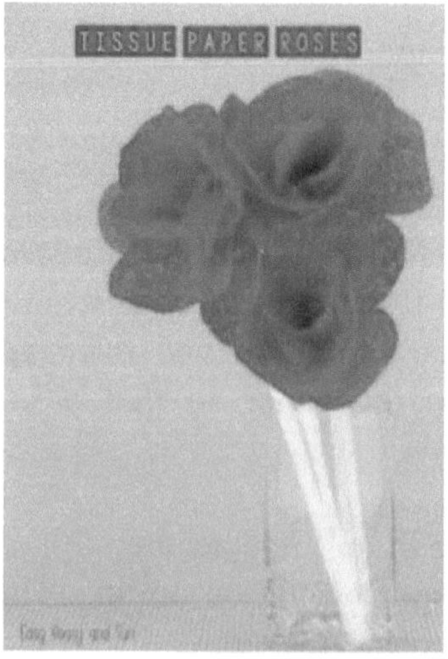

Materials

- Crepe paper (can also use tissue paper or napkins)
- Green drinking straws
- Glue
- Scissors
- Ribbon

Directions

1. Cut out the shapes of 12 petals on the crepe paper but cutting a square at the bottom to serve as the stem. Add a drop of glue to the stem of the first petal and pinch together.

2. Take the next petal and add a drop of glue to the stem and overlapping the first petal, glue together. Continue to do this until you have glued all 12 petals. Make 5" x 1" cuts from the top of the straw downwards so that it looks like a fan.

3. Circle the bottom of the stem with glue and push into the straw - this will support the rose. Tie a ribbon around the bunch of roses and now you have the perfect Mother's Day bouquet.

47. 3-Dimensional Card Flowers

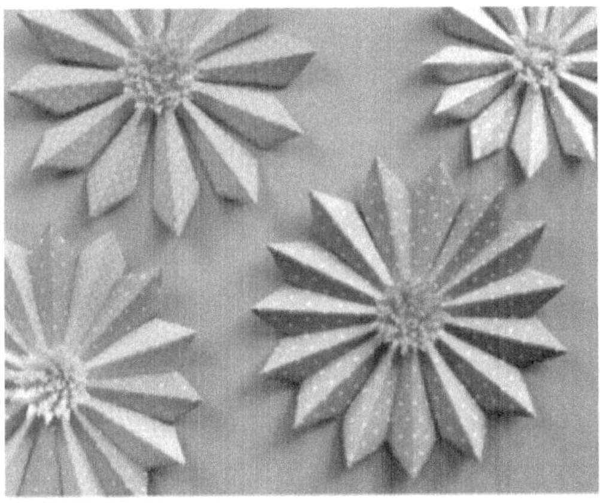

Materials

- Card
- Scissors
- Glue
- Zig zag scissors
- Paper
- Pencil
- Ruler

Directions

1. Draw a triangle to the size of your choice.

2. Trace 12 to 15 triangles onto the card and cut out the shapes. Fold each triangle in half lengthwise and crease well.

3. Fold the two sides at the wide end of the triangle towards the middle fold. Crease well. Overlap the two folded areas and join together with glue.

4. Draw a round circle (1 ½" x 1 ½") on the card and cut out.

5. Place some glue on the circle and attach the tips of the petals. The petals should fan out around the circle like a sun. Cut the edges of the card with zig zag scissors.

6. Draw a line 1/8" from the bottom of the zig zag and cut.

7. Make three strips of 12". Fold down the first 9 triangles so that it makes a ball. Now continue to roll the card dotting with glue at intervals.

8. Gently bend all the triangles outwards. Adhere to the center of your flower. These 3-dimensional flowers look beautiful as table decorations, wall art or as a final topping to gifts.

48. Stained Glass Tissue Paper Flowers

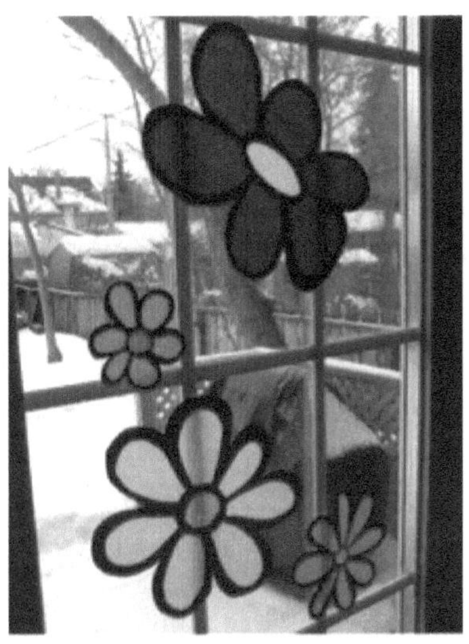

Materials

- Black construction paper
- Tissue paper in different colors
- Pencil crayon
- Scissors
- X-acto blade
- Glue stick

Directions

1. Fold a piece of construction paper in half. Draw the outline of a flower on the paper. Draw a circle in the middle of the flower. Draw an inner outline of the flower.

2. Holding the two pieces of construction paper together cut out the outside line of the flower. Use the x-acto blade to cut the inside shape. You will now have two shapes of the flower and when you overlap them, they will fit perfectly together.

3. Dab some glue along the outline of the flower and paste on the tissue paper. Turn the paper over and cut out the outline of the flower as well as the center hole.

4. Paste a different color tissue paper over the center hole. Paste the other half of the flower outline onto the back of the completed flower. Stick your stained-glass flowers onto the window bringing brightness to a winter's day.

49. Curly Cupcake Liner Flowers

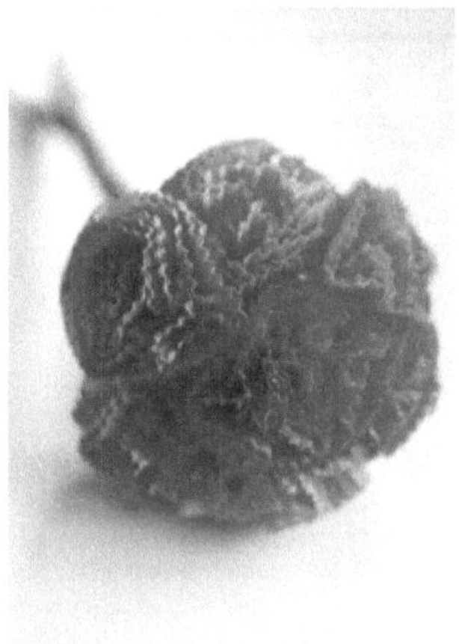

Materials

- Cupcake liners (8 per flower)
- Pipe cleaners
- Floral tape
- Straight pin
- Ribbon (optional)

Directions

1. One can buy either small or large cupcake liners depending on the size of flower you want to make. Remove the cupcake liners from the packet.

2. Flatten 8 cupcake liners with your hands making sure not to remove all the small folds. Place all the cupcake liners on top of one another and with a straight pin, make 2 holes about a ½" apart.

3. Taking 2 cupcake liners at a time, thread the pipe cleaner through the 1 hole from the bottom of the liner. Continue until all 8 cupcake liners are on the pipe cleaner.

4. Bring the pipe cleaner through the 2nd hole and twirl the pipe cleaner to secure. Starting as close as possible to the bottom cupcake liner, wrap the floral tape down the pipe cleaner.

5. Starting with the top cupcake liner, push upwards and pinch the liner between your thumb and index finger. Follow the same method with the rest of the cupcake liners until you have a fluffy flower. To make a beautiful bouquet fit for a bride, join a number of flowers and tie together the stems with a pretty ribbon.

50. Extra-Large Poppies

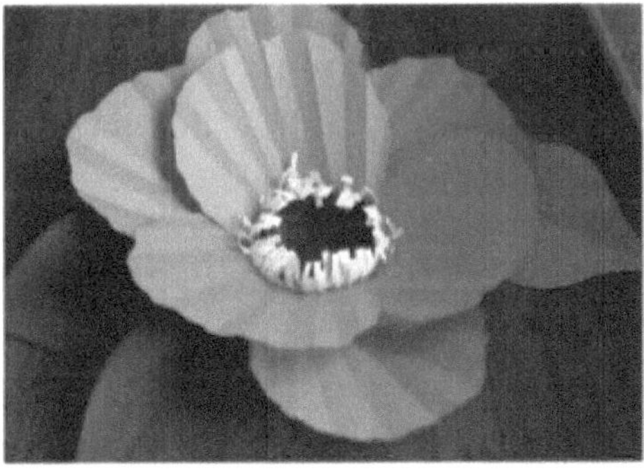

Materials

- 7 Single color sheets of art paper (19" x 25") for the flower
- 1 Sheet yellow art paper for stamen
- 1 Sheet black art paper for center

- 3 Sheets green art paper for leaves (different shades)
- Glue gun
- Pencil
- 18" Ruler
- Compass
- Scissors

Directions

1. Work on a fairly large surface as these flowers are very large and you will need lots of space. Using the short end of the single color (will form the base of the flower), measure 9" from the side and mark with a pencil.

2. On either side of this mark, measure 4 ½" and mark. From the 4 ½" mark start to draw the shape of your flower. It should look like a light bulb or shell, filling the paper. Make the edges slightly wavy and uneven. Cut out and use this as the template for the rest of the petals. At the 9" mark, draw a line horizontally measuring 5" and cut.

3. To create the texture of the petal, start by folding the center of the petal over the ruler. Every 1 – 1 ½" fold the petals over the ruler from the widest edge to the center. Turn over the petal, and fold every 2nd fold in the opposite direction.

4. Run a line of glue on the one side of the 5" cut and glue the 2 sections together. This will give your petal a cup shape. Repeat this process with the rest of the petals. Take 3 petals and glue together so that they form a circle. This will form the center of the flower. Taking the last 4 petals, glue evenly around the center of the flower – this will form the outer petals of the flower.

5. To make the stamen, draw a 16" circle on the yellow paper and cut out. Cut 5" strips all the way around the stamen (they do not all have to be the same width). Curl the strips inwards

with the edge of a closed pair of scissors. Draw a 10" circle on the black piece of paper.

6. Cut 3" strips around the circumference of the circle and curl inwards. Glue the yellow stamen to the center of the flower. Glue the black center onto the yellow stamen. Take the green paper and fold in half lengthwise. Fold either side towards the middle and fold (this will create 2 leaves).

7. Using the fold as the center, draw half the shape of a leaf and cut. Once you unfold the paper you will have the shape of a full leaf. Glue 2 leaves together and glue to the underside of the flower. Make as many leaves as you want and glue to the flower. These extra-large poppies are great to use as center piece decorations.

51. Carnations Made with Tissue Paper

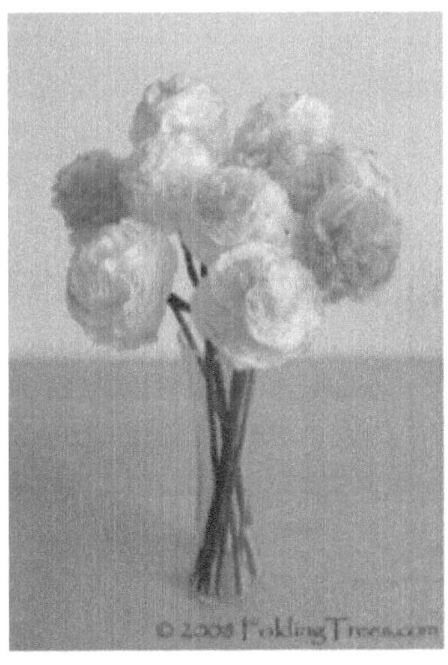

Materials

- Tissue paper
- Scissors
- 2 Large paper clips
- Pipe cleaners

- Floral tape
- Florist wire
- Colored marker pen
- 3" Lid of a circular container
- Large needle
- Vase

Directions

1. Fold the tissue paper in half and again until such time as it fits the size of the lid. Place the lid on the tissue paper and trace around the circumference. Cut out the shape of the lid. Use the paper clips to hold the paper together. Add a second paper clip on the opposite end of the tissue paper.

2. Taking a complimentary color marker, hold the layers of tissue paper together and gently color the edge of the paper. If you hold the paper too firmly, the paper will separate.

3. You may need to color the edges a few times until the paper is saturated with color. Once you reach the paper clip, move the clip to an area where you have already colored and attach. Remove the clips and separate the circles into piles of 8 to 10 circles. Poke two holes through the tissue paper.

4. Fold an inch at the top of the pipe cleaner and insert the long end through the one hole. Insert the folded end through the other hole. Pull the pipe cleaner through and twist underneath the flower (this will secure all the petals). Separate the top petal and crumple upwards towards the center.

5. Crumple the base of the petals and not the inked edges. Continue with the rest of the petals in the same manner. Once all the circles are crumpled, you will end up with a beautiful carnation.

6. Place the florist wire on the pipe cleaner and cut to size. Wind the floral tape around the pipe cleaner and wire.

Arrange the carnations in a vase – you will be surprised to see how natural they look.

52. Tulle and Tissue Paper Flower

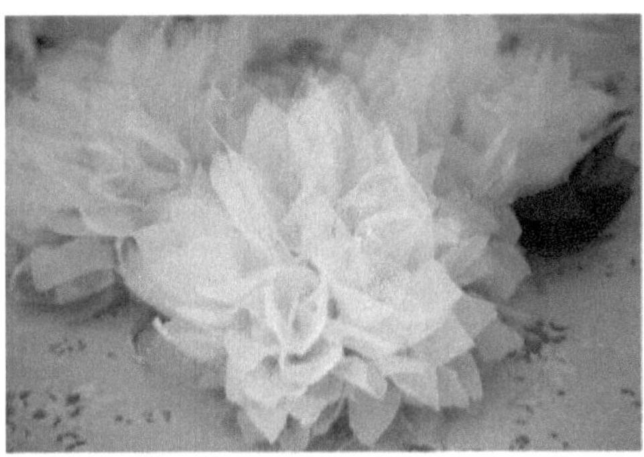

Materials

- Tissue paper (2 colors)
- Tulle
- String
- Scissors

Directions

1. Cut 2 rectangles of each color tissue paper and 2 rectangles of the tulle (the size will depend on the size of the flower required) as long as the rectangles are all the same size. Lay the 4 sheets on top of one another, with the tulle at the top. Line up the edges and fold all the pieces backwards and forwards concertina style.

2. Once you have finished folding, bend the fan in half. Tie tightly with a piece of string. Cut a V shape at the end of each piece making a petal shape.

3. Fan out one side into a half circle and gently start separating the layers lifting them upwards. Unfurl the other side and separate the sections. Gently manipulate the paper into a

flower shape. The addition of the tulle adds pizazz to what could be just an ordinary flower.

53. Flower Pot Center Pieces with Crepe Streamers

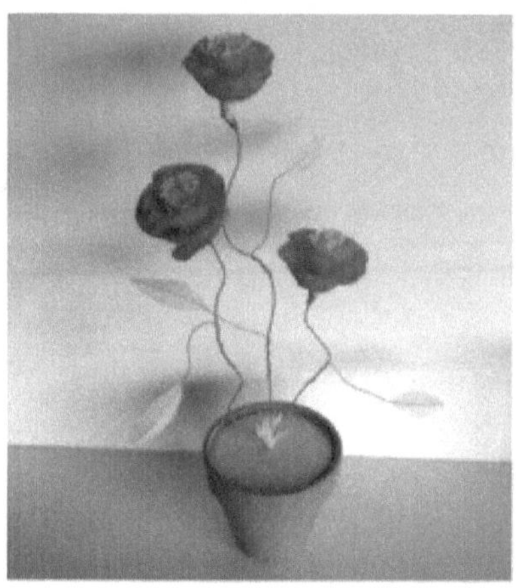

Materials

- Clay pot
- Floral foam
- 22 Gauge cloth covered floral wire
- 32 Gauge cloth covered spool wire
- 3 Colors crepe paper streamers (flower, center and leaves)
- Green felt
- Craft glue
- Acrylic craft paint (optional)
- Scissors
- Knife
- Wire cutters
- Compass
- Ruler
- Large needle

Directions

1. Clean the clay pot (if you have to wash the pot, ensure the pot is completely dry especially if you want to paint the pot). Paint the clay pot (optional can be left in natural state). Cut the floral foam to fit inside the pot. Measure the diameter of the pot.

2. Draw a circle on the felt slightly smaller than the circumference of the pot and cut out. The felt should cover the top and fit just inside the pot. Place on the floral foam and pierce a hole in the center. Glue the felt onto the foam making sure you do not glue over the hole. Allow to dry.

3. Cut a 12" strip of crepe paper streamer (center). Cut fringes along the edges of the paper. Dab the straight edges with spots of glue and wrap a ½" from the top of the floral wire. Pinch the crepe streamer as you wrap. Cut a 24" strip of crepe streamer to make the petals. Cut the edges in a round shape.

4. Dab the edges with spots of glue and start wrapping around the stem. Move the streamer down the base of the stem as you wrap (this will give the petals a more natural look. Cut a 2" strip of crepe streamer paper (green), dab with spot of glue and wrap around the base of the flower. Wrap the spool wire around the area.

5. Draw a leaf shape on the crepe streamer and cut out. Cut a 5" piece of spool wire. Glue the end of the wire to match the length of the leaf and glue onto the leaf. Twist around the wire steam of the flower. Insert the flower into the middle of the clay pot.

6. Using the above directions, make as many flowers as you would like to put into the clay pot. Cut a few inches of green crepe streamer and cut V shapes at the one edge. Dab with a few spots of glue and wrap around the base of the flowers

(will create a grass effect). The flower pots create a great center piece at weddings or parties, and your guests can take them home after the function.

54. Pretty Pink Flowers with A Touch of Glitter

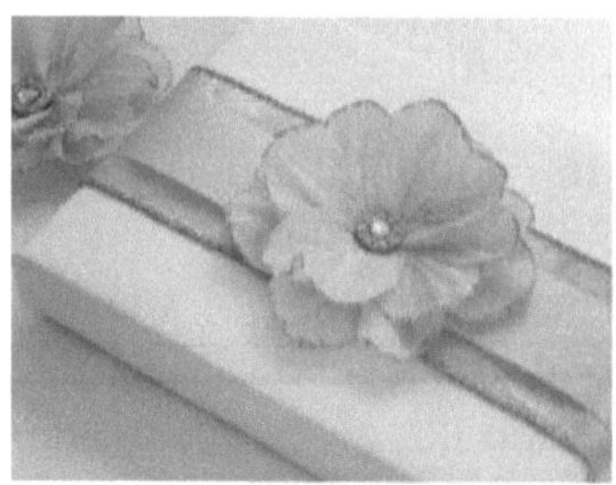

Materials

- Light pink crepe paper streamers
- Pretty button
- Small rhinestone or crystal
- Glue
- Gold or silver glitter
- Card

Directions

1. Cut a 24" length of crepe paper streamer. Fan fold into 8 layers. Cut the edges in a round shape – you will now have 8 petals. Place a thin layer of glue on the button and cover with glitter and place the rhinestone or crystal in the middle.

2. Draw and cut a ½" circle on the card. On a spare piece of card, place a dollop of glue and a pile of glitter. Fold each petal in half and gently dab the edges in glue and then in the glitter. Open up the petals and dry thoroughly. Scrunch up the bottom of the petal and glue onto the card circle. Scrunch up another petal and glue opposite the other petal. Repeat

with two more petals and glue in the blank spaces on the card.

3. Glue the second layer of petals closer to the center, slightly overlapping with the petals below. Do the same with the last two petals. Glue the glittered button to the center of the flower. This flower makes for a beautiful gift embellishment for that extra special friend.

55. Double Crepe Paper Peonies

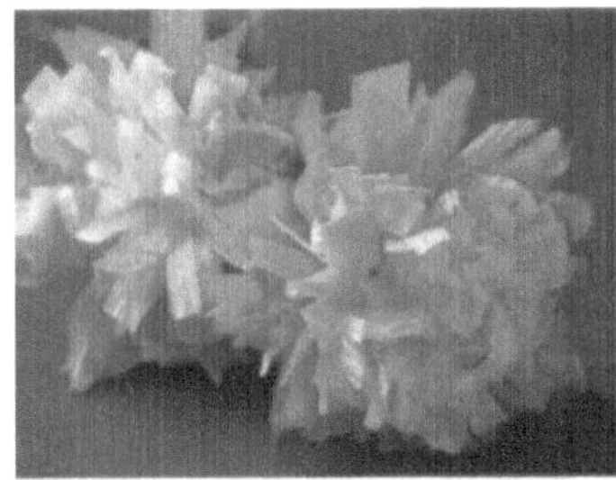

Materials

- Crepe paper (white, light pink and dark pink)
- Green mulberry paper
- Wire
- Glue
- Scissors

Directions

1. Cut 10" strip of the white, light pink and dark pink crepe paper. Cut a 16" strip of dark pink crepe paper. Fold in half each strip of crepe paper 3 times. Using the white crepe paper cut fringes that are 1/8" apart.

2. Cut fringes on the light pink crepe paper ¼" apart. Cut fringes on both dark pink crepe papers 3/8" apart. On the 16" strip of dark pink crepe paper cut off the corner of each

fringe. Cut a piece of wire twice the length of what you would like the flower stem to be.

3. Fold the wire in half and twist the two wires together, leaving a loop in the center (this will prevent the crepe paper from falling off the wire). Unfold each strip of crepe paper and gently wind the white paper around the wire. Glue the end of the paper to the flower.

4. Dab a spot of glue on the flower and start wrapping the light pink crepe paper around the flower securing the end with a dab of glue. Continue with the 10" dark pink crepe paper followed by the 16" piece. Tear a piece of green mulberry paper (width 11").

5. Place a spot of glue on the end and wrap tightly around the base of the flower and continue wrapping down the wire. Tear leaves from the mulberry paper, dab with glue and attach to the stem. Crumple and fluff the petals and voila you have a magnificent peony.

56. Garden Center Pieces with Tissue Paper Flowers

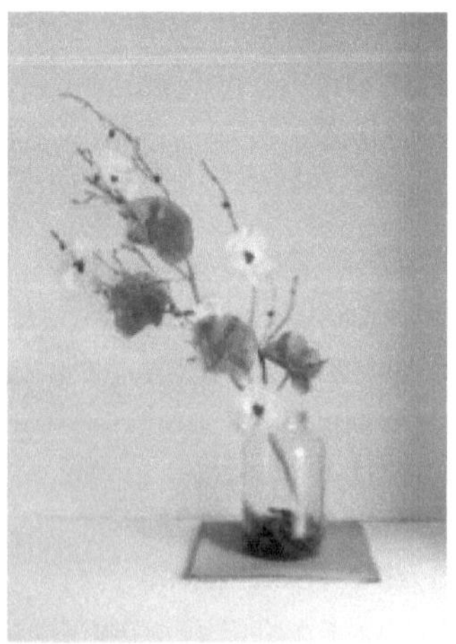

Materials

- Large glass jar
- Sheet moss
- Branches
- Small pompoms
- Tissue paper
- Hot glue gun
- Scissors
- Pencil
- Compass

Directions

1. Fill the bottom of the jar with moss. Place the branches in the jar and trim into the desired shape. Measure and mark 3 different size circles on the tissue paper (cut 4 sheets at a time as this will prevent the tissue paper from tearing).

2. Lay the 3 circles on top of one another – the smallest being on the top. Pinch the tissue paper underneath in the center and gently twist until you get the shape of a flower (this will create a knob underneath the flower which will be used to attach the flower to the branch).

3. Smooth the papers as you twist so that they don't crinkle. Make as many flowers as you need for your centerpiece. Place a dab of glue on the branches and stick the flowers onto the branch. Fresh flowers are very expensive and these center pieces become an inexpensive decoration for your tables.

57. Hanging Rose Balls

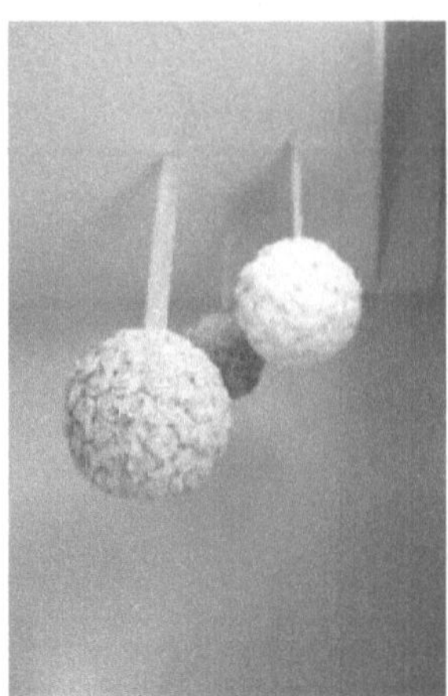

Materials

- Styrofoam balls
- Crepe paper streamers
- Hot glue gun
- Roll of tape
- Ruler
- Ribbon
- Straight pins

Directions

1. Cut crepe paper streamers into 24" strips. Crumple each strip in your hand and then straighten out. Start rolling the crepe paper tightly at first and then loser as you go along so as to give the shape of a rose. Every few inches adhere with a spot of glue and continue rolling and twisting at the same time.

2. Gather the end piece of the crepe paper and stick to the rose. You will need to make numerous roses to cover the Styrofoam ball. Place a roll of tape underneath the ball to prevent it from rolling around.

3. Place a dot of glue underneath the rose and attach to the ball. If the stem is too long, cut it shorter. Continue until you have filled the whole ball.

4. Cut a piece of ribbon to the required length and attach to the ball with straight pins. You can make rose balls in different sizes and they look gorgeous suspended from the ceiling.

58. Quick and Easy Paper Flower Center Pieces

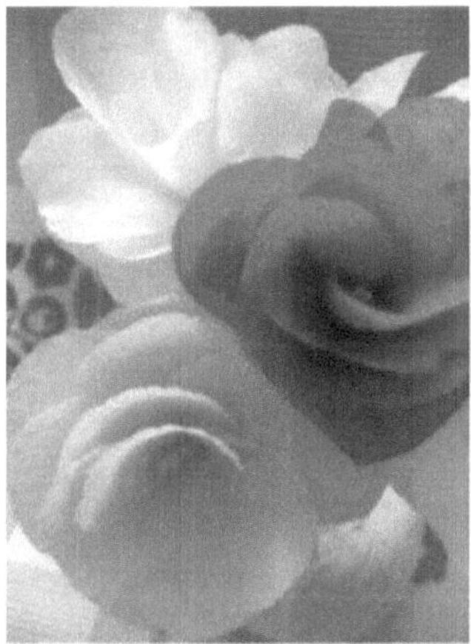

Materials

- Crepe paper or tissue paper
- 18" Gauge paper stem wires
- ½" Floral tape
- Wire cutters
- Scissors
- Glue
- Vase

Directions

1. Cut a wire stem 8 to 10" long. Cut the tissue paper or crepe paper in strips of 1 ½". Cut a short piece of yellow paper (to

make the stamen) and place a line of glue on either side of the wire stem.

2. Turn the paper over the wire stem. Place a line of glue over the glued paper, roll around the stem and glue closed. Using a contrasting color cut a strip of paper 1 ½" wide.

3. Fold the paper in half and in half again until you have approximately 12 sheets. Cut out the shape of a petal leaving the bottom straight.

4. Place a line of glue along the bottom of the paper and glue over the side of the yellow stamen. Continue to glue the petals around the flower, pinching the petals as you attach to the flower. Open the petals according to the shape you want.

5. Attach the floral tape under the flower and wind down the length of the stem. Slightly bend the flower stems and arrange in a vase. You can also insert into a ball of yarn or a jar full of buttons depending on the occasion.

59. Double Fringed Paper Flowers

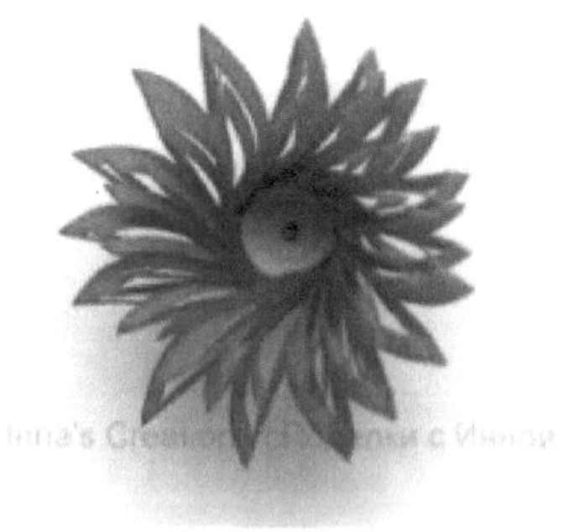

Materials

- Colored paper (double sided)
- Yellow paper

* Glue
* Scissors
* Toothpick or skewer or quilling tool
* Ruler
* Marker

Directions

1. Measure and mark a strip of paper 1" wide and 4" long. Cut the paper. Fold the paper in half lengthwise. At a 45-degree angle cut fringes over the folded edge of the card, leaving a space of 1/8" at the bottom.

2. To make the center of the flower, cut a piece of yellow paper 1/8" wide by 10" long.

3. Glue the yellow strip to the bottom end of the strip. Using the toothpick/skewer/quilling tool tightly roll up the yellow paper.

4. Dab a spot of glue between the yellow paper and the beginning of the petals. This will ensure that the inner coil remains in place. Continue rolling up the rest of the flower, placing a spot of glue at regular intervals. The petals will automatically fluff up as you wind.

5. Once completed, dab a spot of glue on the edge of the petal and hold firmly to dry. Attach the flower to greeting cards or scrapbook picture frames.

60. Fluffy Quilled Paper Flowers

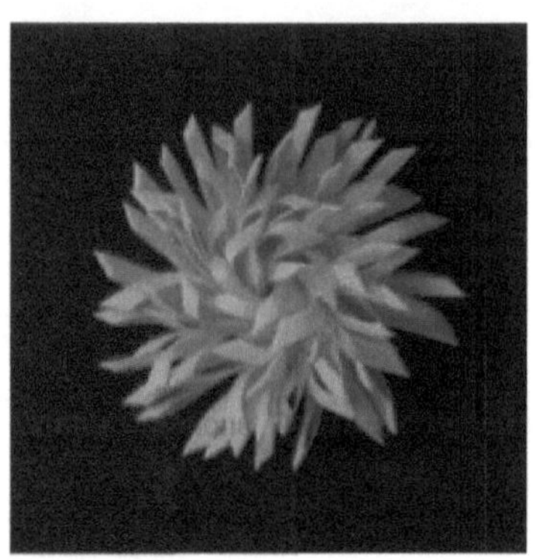

Materials

- Double sided colored paper
- Glue
- Scissors
- Ruler
- Marker

Directions

1. Measure and mark the paper 1" x 12" and cut. Fold the paper in half (lengthwise). At a 45-degree angle, cut fringes in the paper leaving a space of 1/8" at the bottom edge.

2. With the quilling tool start to roll the card, putting a spot of glue as the paper meets. Roll tightly and once at the end, secure with glue.

3. Different thicknesses and types of paper can be used although if too thick or heavy the paper will be difficult to roll. The fluffy flower makes for beautiful gift embellishments.

61. Colorful Paper Dahlia Wreath

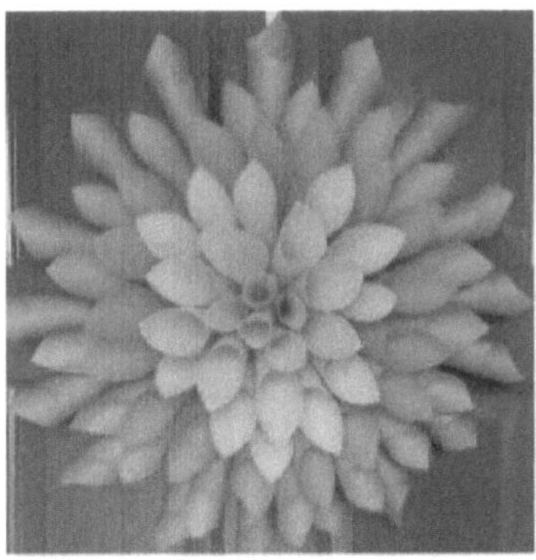

Materials

- Thick cardboard
- 25-30 Pieces of 12" x 12" cardstock (3 colors)
- Ribbon for hanging
- Hot glue gun
- Scissors
- Ruler
- Marker

Directions

1. Depending on the size of the wreath you require, one can either leave the paper size as is or you can make smaller. Roll each piece of paper in the shape of a cone making sure that the one corner is fairly open at the top as this will be the open side of the petal.

2. Run a line of hot glue along the edge and seal. This will ensure that you retain the cone shape. For the outer edge as well as the next two layers of petals, you will need 17 cones per circle. The number of inner petals will be less, depending on how closely you glue the petals.

3. Measure and cut out a 9" circle in the thick cardboard. You can use a cereal box instead of purchasing thick card. Flatten and fold ½" from the bottom edge of the cone.

4. Put a small amount of glue on the flattened piece and stick the cone to the outer edge of the circle. Leave a small gap between each cone. Continue this process until the outer edge is completely surrounded by cones.

5. Now do the same with the next layer but paste the cones further into the circle and not on the flattened sections of the previous cones. Make sure that the layer of cones is positioned in between the heads of the previous cones. Keep going until you reach the center of the cone. All that's left is to glue a piece of ribbon to the back of the circle and hang on the door.

62. Felt Rose Gift Decorations

Materials

- Felt
- Hot glue gun
- Scissors
- Marker

Directions

1. Draw a spiral circle on the piece of felt. Cut out along the marked lines leaving a circle at the end. You will be left with a long spiral of fabric.

2. Leaving the circle to the outside, tightly roll the felt (center) making the roll less tight towards the end as this will allow the petals to be more rose like. Place a spot of glue at intervals. Dab a spot of glue at the end to secure.

3. Fill the inner part of the petal with glue and attach the circle. This will give your rose a more finished look and will also help to keep the flowers together. Cut out a few green felt leaves and arrange together with the roses to decorate gifts.

63. Button Poppies

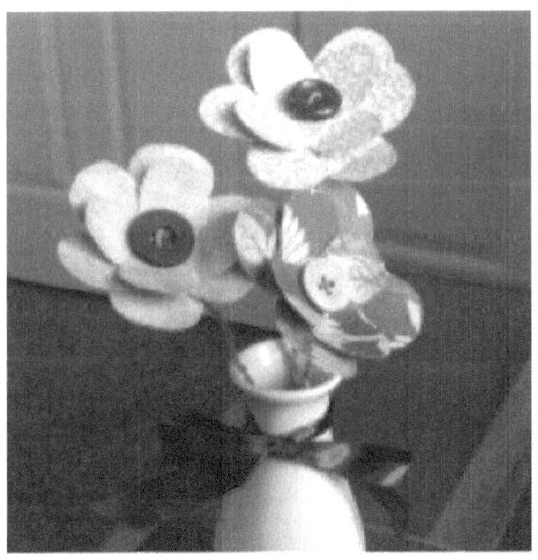

Materials

- Double sided patterned card
- Covered florist wire
- Pencil
- 1/8" Hole punch

- Vase
- Ribbon

Directions

1. Draw 3 figure 8 shapes on the patterned card (3.5" wide by 2.5" long). Draw 2 figure 8 shapes on the patterned card (3.5" wide by 1.5" long).

2. When you cut out the shapes, make sure that you leave enough space in the middle to punch 2 holes. Starting with the 3 larger shapes, place them on top of one another so that the petals slightly offset one another.

3. Add the 2 smaller shapes on top in the same format. Punch 2 holes through the center section of the stack. Gently push the florist wire through the 1 hole from the underneath side of the stack to the top.

4. Thread on a button. Turn the wire and thread through the next hole of the button and through your flower. Twist the floral tape underneath the flower to secure. Arrange the button poppies in a vase and tie a complimentary ribbon around your vase.

64. Tissue Paper Floral Wreath

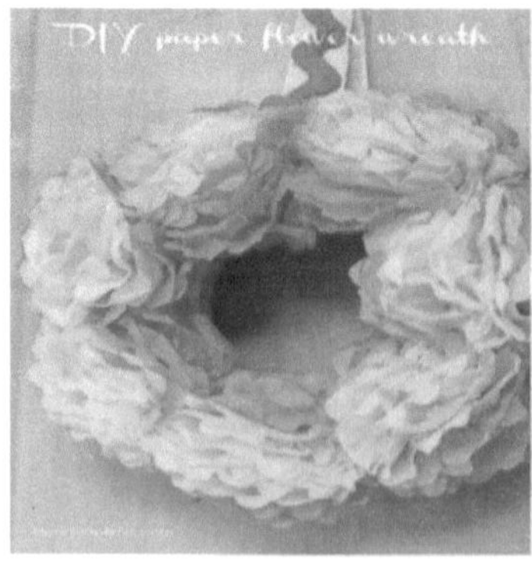

Materials

- Pack of tissue paper
- Scissors
- Floral wire
- Wire cutters
- Foam wreath
- Fabric or ribbon
- Hot glue gun

Directions

1. Fold the pack of tissue paper in half and cut an 8 x 8" square (you will end up with 16 layers of tissue paper). Fold the tissue paper in 1" folds accordion style. Wrap a piece of floral wire in the middle of the flower and cut off the wire. Cut a round edge on each side of the tissue paper. Gently pull each layer of flower towards the wire and fluff. Wrap the foam wreath with matching fabric or ribbon.

2. Loop a piece of ribbon around the wreath to hang. Hot glue each flower to the wreath. Hang the floral wreath to a door which will provide a warm and colorful welcome to your guests.

65. Paper Flower Gift Tags

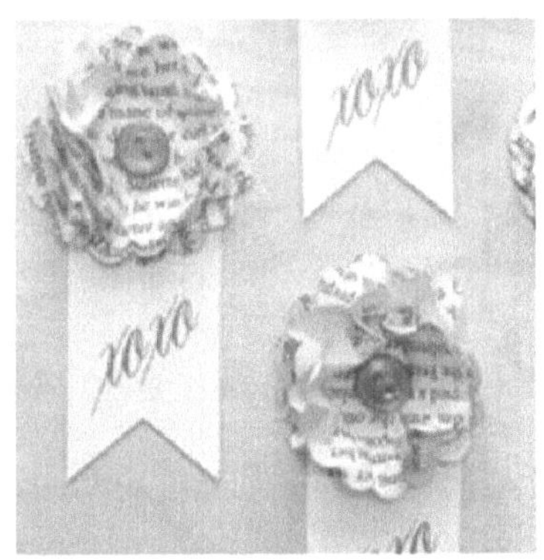

Materials

- Pages from an old book
- Flower shape punch cutter
- Chart card
- Awl tool
- Brad fastener
- Scissors
- Buttons
- Ruler
- Pencil
- Glue

Directions

1. Cut 5 petals with the punch cutter. Measure and mark a rectangular shape on the card (1" by 3") and cut out the shape. Cut a V shape at the bottom of the card. Layer the petal and place on top of the rectangular card. Make a small hole though the petals and the card. Gently push a brad through the top of the petals and fasten underneath the card.

2. One at a time, scrunch the edges of the petals. Glue a button to the center of the flower. Write a message onto the tag and attach to gift packages.

66. Giant Yellow Sunflower

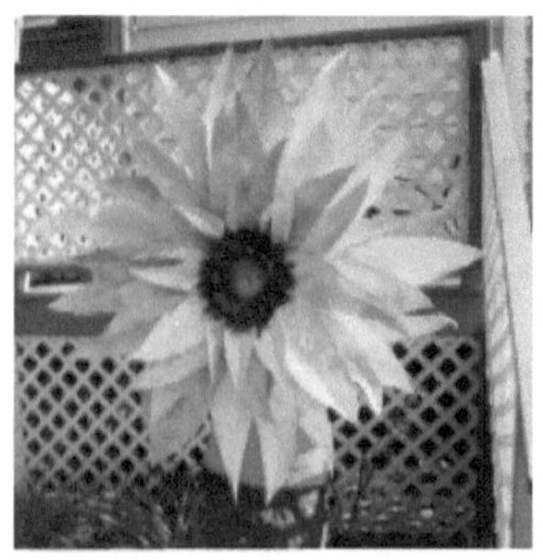

Materials

- Thick brown craft paper
- Different colors of latex paint (red, orange, yellow, brown etc.)
- Sponge or roller
- Pencil
- Scissors
- Hot glue gun
- 1 Round platter size lightweight / paper plate or wicker basket
- 1 Round dinner size lightweight / paper plate

Directions

1. This flower is extremely large and you will have to use at least 3 sheets of craft paper. Have fun and paint the craft paper in various shades of yellow paint. Keep some scrap pieces to paint in brown (inside section of the flower).

2. Fold the painted craft paper in half and draw long oval shapes in 5 different sizes. You will need in the region of 100 petals. For the center of the flower cut out 3 large brown circles and cut fringes on the edges, leave a circle shape in the middle. Cut the edge of the fringes at different angles and fold up the edges. Dab spots of glue in the center and stack the 3 fringed circles inside one another.

3. For the center of the flower, cut a smaller circle in a different color. Fringe the edges of the circle and fold all the fringes to the inside. The shape will look something like a ball.

4. Add the ball to the middle of the brown fringed center piece and glue securely. Turn the platter or wicker basket upside down and hot glue half of the petals onto the platter or wicker basket. Using the dinner paper plate right side up, hot glue the remaining petals onto the plate.

5. Spread hot glue over the bottom of the dinner plate and stick onto the first tier of petals that you made. Take the stack of brown fringes and hot glue to the middle of the flower. Fluff the fringes at different angles to get a ruffled and untidy look. Hang or place your giant yellow sunflower in a place of prominence, its sunshine colors giving a warm welcome to the room and guests.

67. Daffodils Made with Cupcake Liners

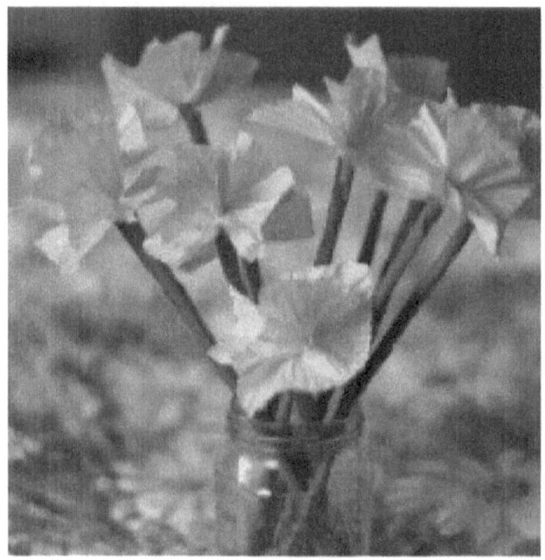

Materials

- Yellow cupcake liners (two shades)
- Plastic drinking straws
- Frog tape or floral tape
- Scissors
- Vase or jar

Directions

1. Divide the cupcake liners into two piles, one pile for the outer petal and the other for the inner petal. Take the outer cupcake liners and fold in thirds. Making a curved V, cut the rounded edges of the cupcake liner. Cut a small slit in the

middle of the liner. The liner will now look like a 6-pointed star.

2. Using your thumb and forefinger pinch the middle of the inner cupcake liner and push through the slit in the outer layer cupcake liner. Pinch the two cupcake liners together and secure the first inch of the liners with frog or floral tape.

3. Insert the drinking straw to the tape and base of the liners and wind the tape around the drinking straw. Pull the outer petal downwards and the inner petal upwards. Cut the straws to different lengths according to the size of the vase and arrange the daffodils.

68. Garland of Paper Doily Flowers

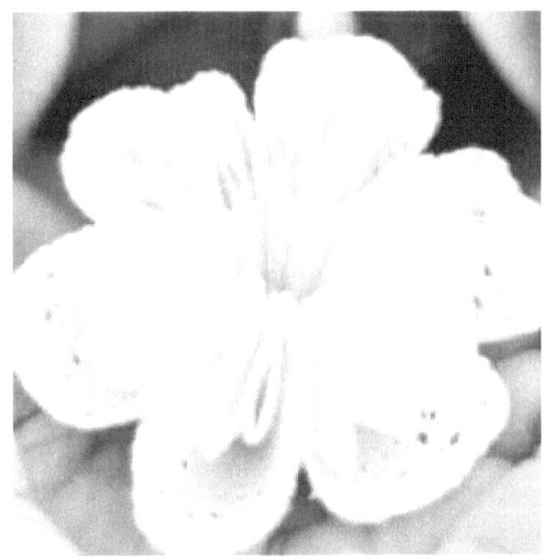

Materials

- Paper doilies
- Hot glue gun
- Tea (can be rooibos or black tea)
- Shallow pan
- Thick brown floral wire

Directions

1. Fold the doily in half. Fold both corners to the center of the doily (you will have a diamond shape). From the center, fold each half towards the edge of the doily. Open both corners and fold flat. Each flower will need 6 doily petals. If you want different size flowers use a variety of doily sizes.

2. Place the doilies in a shallow pan and cover with the tea. The color of the doilies will depend on the strength of the tea made or the type of tea used. Let the doilies soak for about 15 minutes.

3. Take out the doilies and allow to dry overnight. Fold the edges of the doily towards the center and you will have a petal shape. Run a line of glue along the edge of the large petals and press the other edge firmly together. Smaller petals will need a dot of glue.

4. Place a large dot of glue under the lace of petal one and firmly press the next petal to the glue dot. Hold in place until secure. Continue attaching the next three petals in the same way.

5. To attach the sixth petal, dab a spot of glue under the lace of petal one and five. Attach both sides until secure, this is the petal that will hold your flower together. If you want to brighten up a party venue, these flowers can be used to make a beautiful garland.

6. Measure the length of the floral wire required. Turn the flowers upside down. Place a huge dollop of glue on the wire and attach the first flower. Hold in place until the glue turns white. Continue with the next flower until you have attached all the flowers. Hang the garland in the chosen area or can be used as part of your table decorations.

Conclusion

Fresh flowers are beautiful. But paper flowers last forever. Take the time, develop this skill, and learn new and wonderful ways to bring about the beauty of creations in no time.

You will add beautiful touches to your gifts and to your home and these beautiful additions will last a very long time.

You might need to buy some supplies, but that is all that is needed. And the maintenance of these flowers will be considerably lower than any of the fresh creations that you can buy.

You can change the arrangements as often as you like without worrying about the expense of doing so – match your flowers to your mood, the occasion or your décor – it's all up to you.

You can really learn a lot from this craft, and you can even turn it into a business. Even if you are not business minded though, you can find hours of joy in bringing the spring out of any arrangement, even when fresh flowers are not available.

Happy crafting…

Last Chance to Get YOUR Bonus!

FOR A LIMITED TIME ONLY – Get my best-selling book "DIY Crafts: The 100 Most Popular Crafts & Projects That Make Your Life Easier" absolutely FREE!

Readers who have downloaded the bonus book as well have seen the greatest changes in their crafting abilities and have expanded their repertoire of crafts – so it is *highly recommended* to get this bonus book today!

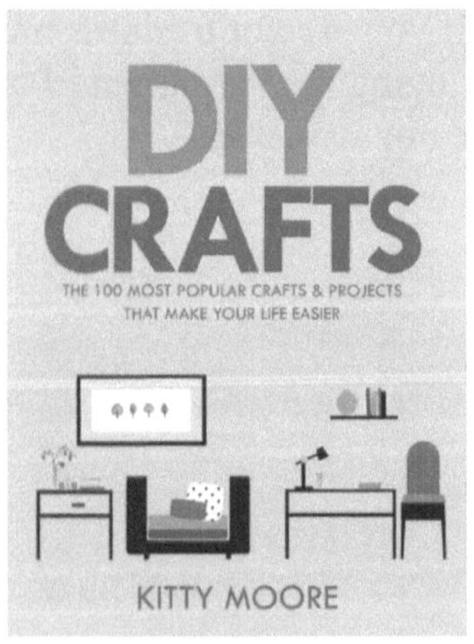

Get your free copy at:

ArtsCraftsAndMore.com/Bonus

Final Words

Thank you for downloading this book!

I really hope that you have been inspired to create your own projects and that you will have a lot of fun crafting.

I do hope that you and your family have found lots of ways to fill lazy afternoons or rainy days in a more fun way.

If you have enjoyed this book and would like to share your positive thoughts, could you please take 30 seconds of your time to go back and give me a review on my Amazon book page!

I really appreciate these reviews because I like to know what people have thought about the book.

Again, thank you and have fun crafting!

Disclaimer

No Warranties: The authors and publishers don't guarantee or warrant the quality, accuracy, completeness, timeliness, appropriateness or suitability of the information in this book, or of any product or services referenced by this site.

The information in this site is provided on an "as is" basis and the authors and publishers make no representations or warranties of any kind with respect to this information. This site may contain inaccuracies, typographical errors, or other errors.

Liability Disclaimer: The publishers, authors, and other parties involved in the creation, production, provision of information, or delivery of this site specifically disclaim any responsibility, and shall not be held liable for any damages, claims, injuries, losses, liabilities, costs, or obligations including any direct, indirect, special, incidental, or consequences damages (collectively known as "Damages") whatsoever and howsoever caused, arising out of, or in connection with the use or misuse of the site and the information contained within it, whether such Damages arise in contract, tort, negligence, equity, statute law, or by way of other legal theory.

www.ingramcontent.com/pod-product-compliance
Lightning Source LLC
Chambersburg PA
CBHW031357060726
47590CB00007B/2818